THE ROAD LESS-TRAVELED OFTEN INVOLVES SMACKING FACE-FIRST THROUGH SPIDER WEBS

A Life of Animal Encounters

by
Sandy Carlson

The Merry Viking Publishing House LLC

ISBN-13: 978-1981556113
ISBN-10: 1981556117

DEDICATED TO:

Naomi, Matthew & Isabel

ACKNOWLEDGEMENTS:

For my adventuresome family who loves the outdoors, and thanks be to God who created us all.

Several of these stories were first written in either the weekly Sand Castles articles for the *Battle Creek Enquirer* (2005-2007) or on Sandy Carlson's blog, re-written to fit this format.

1. Honeymoon in the Ozarks
2. Ohio Snakes
3. Grandmother's Cottage, Part I
4. "Don't move!"
5. First Time Fishing
6. Turtle Cleanup
7. Alligator in the Northern Lake
8. My First Rodeo
9. Deer, Oh, Deer!
10. Swimming Deer in Michigan
11. Black Cats…or not!
12. South Dakota Fletcher
13. Pitbulls and Puppies
14. Carlson-Stark Pets
15. My Pet Rabbit
16. LuLu the Elephant
17. Creatures in a Rowboat
18. Roosters
19. Down on the Farm
20. Grandmother's Cottage, Part II
21. Bird and Animal Sanctuaries
22. Undomesticated Dogs
23. More Dogs, Unleashed
24. Things That Go Swoop in the Night
25. Chatter Around the Pup
26. It's a Trap!
27. Squirrels
28. Wisconsin Roundup
29. Wisconsin Farm Hand
30. Up to Bat
31. More About Bats
32. Flying Trail Map

33. Chipmunk Horrors
34. Algonquin Provincial Park, 1987-1996
35. Algonquin Wolf Howls and a BBC Documentary
36. Moose Sightings in Algonquin
37. Bear in Algonquin
38. Father-Daughter Trip to Canada
39. New Cats, Old Cat, and a Dog
40. Aliens
41. Bandits, Part I
42. Bandits, Part II
43. Bandits, Part III
44. Wildfire Herd
45. Horses, of Courses
46. Dakota Steeds
47. Shaker Day Camp Horses and Dragons
48. Backpaddling off the Erie Canal
49. Williamsville Fowls
50. Rural Northern Illinois
51. Dusky Company
52. South Dakota Miller Moth Invasion
53. French Creek Backpacking
54. Black Hills Bison (and a few burros)
55. Silly Bison Question
56. Annual Buffalo Roundups
57. South Dakota Pretty Ladies
58. South Dakota Roundup #1
59. South Dakota Roundup #2
60. Birds, Birds, everywhere
61. 2011 Storm Effect on Animals
62. Bee Powerful

63. Yellowstone Wildlife
64. Sunset in Yellowstone
65. Squeaky Encounters
66. My Pet Mouse
67. Children's Garden Mice
68. Red Worms
69. Wisconsin Snakes
70. Salted Nuts
71. Murder!
72. Deer Hunting with the Carlson Men
73. Tick-Tock-Ticks
74. More Little Guys
75. South Dakota Rattlers
76. Reptile Gardens Research
77. Little Piney Three Ravine
78. Snaky P.S.
79. Roadkill
80. The Other Snakes and Such
81. More Encounters

We Carlsons like to hike. When camping, we tented.

We appreciate God's variety in the great outdoors. We have learned that hiking the trails less traveled by people includes not only spotting animals in the wild, but that the leader often breaks the trail with a spider web strand across her face or arms, and hoping the spider who wove it was not in the middle of the web.

We have experienced many animals through the years, from those as small as seed ticks in Arkansas to charging bison in South Dakota, as well as the other animals, encounters with domesticated types.

Our wild animal "cousins," are usually predictable. If they are hungry, they seek food. If they have horns or teeth or claws or stingers, they know how to use them. Although we've hiked in bear country, and seen several, we have never carried pepper spray. We've learned when to approach, when to stop, or when to slowly back away.

We live alongside other creatures on this earth the same as we do with people, with love and patience and knowledge and gentleness and respect, knowing we are all created by one God.

Chapter One – Honeymoon in the Ozarks

Before we married in Wisconsin (1978), Jeff decided that for our honeymoon we should take the summer off. He was a seminary student. I was a teacher. He reasoned there would never be that long a stretch of time off work for us until our far-off retirement. (His prediction has proved true.)

As we had little money between us, we chose to camp. Family hotels back then were a whopping $12-$20 a night; campgrounds were $6; National Forest campgrounds were $2/night; and backpacking country was free. We spent less than $2,000 for our seven-week honeymoon—about half of it on car repairs.

We packed my 1974 Ford Pinto with: two tents (a 3-person canvas one for regular campgrounds and a nylon pup tent for backpacking), a blow-up raft with oars, my guitar, two suitcases, two backpacks, two sleeping bags, a four-can cooler, several books, cameras and rolls of film, and two boxes of dried food along with a "kitchen box" holding pans and utensils. And off we went.

By our fifth night, we were exhausted with noisy campground people, so decided to backpack into the Ozark Mountains of Arkansas—in Tom Sawyer National Forest. A park ranger gave us instructions to some out-of-the-way locations. We cruised down the highway, up an abandoned dirt road for a few miles, and then parked as far off the road as we could, next to the trees. We shouldered our packs and took off down a narrow path, which we later figured must have been a fire road. We hiked for a couple of hours through the dense woods until we came to a meadow in a large valley basin. From the blackened stumps and knee-high grass, we knew it was the location of an earlier forest fire, perhaps a year or two before.

We walked to the far end of the meadow trying to find where the trail would go out of the basin. We couldn't find any. Perhaps there was none. Tired, hot, and wanting to decide what to do next, we sat on a fallen tree trunk along the forest's edge and ate GORP (Good Old Raisins and Peanuts, with a few M&M's tossed in) as a lunch break. It didn't take long before both of us started itching. Crawling over our exposed hands and necks were teeny tiny bugs. There were thousands of them. Each insect, smaller than the head of a pin. Crawling, crawling over us.

We jumped off the log, brushed off as many of them as we could, but quickly realized they had crawled under our clothing, even our underwear. We snatched our backpacks and ran into the meadow where there weren't rotting logs or overhanging tree branches for any more of the little guys to drop on us.

Less than a week married, and here we stood in the middle of a National Forest meadow, butt-naked, brushing bugs off ourselves or each other's body where we couldn't reach.

By this time, some of the ticks had dug into our skin. We then killed six of them at a time with one hot-but-blown-out match, their tiny bodies snapping, before the match was too cool to be effective.

We used up four books of matches, or about eighty individual sticks, burning them off. (A few years later we found out the name of this particular bug: seed ticks. Well named.)

The ticks discouraged us from spending the night in the woods, where we assumed there would be literally billions more of the tiny critters. We moved away from the tick death zone (for some might have survived in the grass) to the middle of the meadow, far from where we had brushed them off. We stomped down the grass in a wide circle, and set up our little orange nylon backpacking tent in the center.

I didn't know what wild animals occupied the Ozarks, and felt vulnerable and new-bride nervous in this wide, exposed meadow. I'd read how dogs marked their territory to keep other dogs away. My new-groom complied to the request of his tick-frightened bride to do the same around our tent area.

There was no safe place for a fire, so we used canned heat to cook our supper. With no campfire to keep us awake, as soon as it got dark, we entered our small tent. It was called a "two-person tent," but only if you were skinny people, and only if you lay on your sides.

A couple hours later, in the pitch black, I was awakened by a noise. It first sounded like a herd of deer running through the meadow, right towards us. Then they stopped. Silence.

I tried to see Jeff but couldn't tell in the dark if he was sleeping.

Then, starting from up the far hill, I heard that sound again, once more charging and stopping just ten feet from our tent where it, whatever it was, stomped and snorted.

At least this time I was able to determine there was only one of something. The charging, snorting and stomping repeated several times. We newlyweds silently endured this torment for about an hour. A fact we concurred in the morning. It's interesting how in these situations, you really have the urge to urinate, but really-really don't want to make the tiniest rustle of your sleeping bag to alert the animal of your presence, let alone step outside the thin wall of the tent.

The next morning as we discussed the night noises, I discovered I wasn't the only one who was thinking "Bigfoot." In the dark, going through the ordeal, neither of us felt safe to speak or even whisper. We determined it was a hoofed animal and very large, but not a deer which moves quietly through woods even when running.

Several years later we described this event to a man from Arkansas. He immediately flung wide open his eyes and identified the creature: a wild boar. "Groups of hunters go after them. Every year someone dies from a boar attack. You were very, very lucky." In reality, we knew it was God's providence that we had brought plenty of water, and one of us who could widely "mark our territory," which we believed kept the night beast out those ten feet from our tent.

Snakes have rather followed me wherever I go.

It's not so much that I'm terrified of snakes, as that they startle me with their non-mammal slithering at shoe level (I'd always say).

When the four of us hiked, I'd normally lead, the boys would be in the middle, and Jeff would make sure no curious boy got left behind. Consequently, I was often the first Carlson to spot the slithering reptile. I'd yelp, leap, and run back, while my three guys rushed around me, asking, "Where? Where? Where?"

***

My maternal grandparents owned two hundred acres of farm and woodland in southern Ohio, Colrain, fairly across the river from Wheeling, West Virginia. The farm animals included cows, a bull, pigs, chickens and rooster (of course), nasty, red-toothed nutria (for a few years), a dozen barn cats, one house cat, one friendly dog, and a mean old dog who hated everyone.

Since there were no cable channels, no video games or hand-held devises, we kids were on our own outside, which was most of the time while down on the farm. There were only three TV channels anywhere in America at that time, in black and white, and the reception in those southern hills was always snowy. It was more like a mystery watching TV there, trying to decipher what was going on, or even what program it might be. For this very reason, we spent a lot of our time on the farm outside.

***

One time, down on the farm, I was set to go play outside after lunch. Everyone else was still at the table. As I stood with my hand on the front door handle, a monstrous black snake prevented me from leaving. It stretched across the entire width of their twelve-foot-wide porch. I couldn't see the tail nor head. I returned to the dining room where everyone was eating or talking, and politely waited for a break in the conversation to inform them of my find. Manners.

Not a person believed me…because they all knew me, and I wasn't being my typical hysterical at spotting a snake. When I persisted, Granddad finally took a peek. He told us all to remain in the house while he grabbed his gun and went out the back door. He called for his snake-killing dog, who didn't like kids too much, either. When the others looked out the front windows, a couple of them saw a tail slide off the porch. At least Granddad had seen the monster.

A few minutes later, we heard barking followed by gun shots. Several gun shots. A while later, Granddad returned and hung up his gun. When others asked him how big the snake actually was, all he answered was, "Big."

***

On this farm was a pond in the middle of the cow pasture downhill from the house. There was a rickety old dock with missing boards which extended onto the water. It wasn't unusual for snakes to be around the pond, either. But with a swimming coach for a father, we three kids liked swimming anytime, anywhere. Once, Dad spotted a water moccasin swimming along with us, several feet away. Dad yelled: "Clear the pool!" Swim time was over.

Of course, during our swim, the cows might wander over. My dad was terrified of the big animals, so we never stayed in the pond after a single cow was spotted wandering in our direction. But if the bull was seen, Dad ran up the hill first "to hold the gate open" for us kids who yelled and swung our towels around, trying to catch up to him.

***

Snake don't limit themselves to farms in Ohio. I went to Shaker Day Camp for a few weeks each summer, "guest" of a family friend who owned the camp. I loved being outdoors, and loved going barefoot. (Still do.) On camp days, I would usually only wear shoes on the bus rides there and home again. Bus floors are gross. I also knew the camp area very well, and was often the leader through the wooded trails. There were teensy red spiders, thumbnail-sized tree toads, and in the creek, crawfish. Of course, there were snakes. Being the leader, I had the opportunity to spot the snakes first. Once I stepped on one in my bare foot. At the pressure, it wound itself around my leg. The entire line of girls behind screamed right along with me.

***

17

When I was in college, my parents moved to three acres across the street from the Cuyahoga Park System. At that time, they had a cat named Tiger. Home for summer, Mom wanted to get a picture of me sitting on their lawn with the cat. I refused. I already knew Tiger collected prizes to bring home to her—mice, birds, snakes—most of the time they were dead. I didn't want to have any snake in the photo with me. Mom poo-pooed the idea long enough that I finally gave in.

So, I sat on the front lawn, with Tiger on my lap, when I felt a movement. I looked down to see a snake had also climbed onto my lap. I threw the cat into the air and ran for the house. My mother, still laughing, came inside and told me she'd gotten rid of the snake, but no matter how many times she said that, picture-taking was done for the day.

Chapter Three – Grandmother's Cottage, Part I

My paternal grandmother owned a cottage at Devils Lake, Michigan, about fifteen miles from her home in Adrian. Our Cleveland family of five would go there for the last week or two of August, depending on who had a job back in Ohio. Pre-interstate days, it would take about five hours to drive there. We kids had free range, except for two times during each cottage stay. One was to have all the great-aunties come out for a sweet corn dinner. The other was the snapping turtle hunt.

On a specific morning Dad would take us on the raft, a.k.a. pontoon boat today, across the lake to the sandbar. We would cruise the two- to three-feet deep waters looking for snapping turtles. When someone spotted one either my dad or brother would jump in and grab it by the sides and put it onto the pontoon boat in a special wired area we made for them. After we captured eight or fifteen turtles, we'd head back across the lake to our cottage. We kept the turtles in another wired area overnight near the dock. In the morning, my dad and brother would release them, and we'd stand on the dock watching them swim back toward the sandbar. I always felt glad to see them swimming home, and not being within toe-snapping proximity.

***

One early morning, only one, my dad took my brother and me in a rowboat to the drop off spot several cottages down. We put in our fishing lines and for fifteen minutes caught nothing. So dad rowed back to the cottage. But we did do a lot of other water sports.

I tried my hand at fishing many long minutes after that experience—using a safety pin tied to the end of a string which I dangled in the water. I didn't use any bait, though. I didn't catch any fish, either. Maybe, like my dad, I didn't have the patience to be a fisherman.

***

I'd go out alone in the canoe, paddling from the bow while sitting on the little triangular metal overhang. I'd dangle my feet in the water, and look for signs of clams. When I found a twisting trail through the sandy bottom I would slowly follow it with the canoe until the trail disappeared. I knew there would be a clam down there but I left it alone.

***

Roger found a vole one summer. He wanted to keep it as a pet. He put it in a wired fence at the back of the cottage. In the morning, the vole was gone. It did didn't take us long to figure out how. The hole through the dirt and under that little wire fence told all.

Chapter Four – "Don't Move!"

When Jeff and I had been married only a few months, we lived in NW Illinois. I was awakened in the middle of the night by some peculiar new-husband behavior. There, in the dark, Jeff slapped his chest a few times, then lay still. I thought it was a nightmare, so started back to sleep. But then came some more chest-slapping along with striking at his pillow. I scooted over a bit, wanting to avoid this very physical nightmare. He lay still once more, and I attempted, not very successfully, to get back to sleep. Suddenly, Jeff stood straight up next to the bed and turned on the light, staring at me. I raised my eyebrows at him questioningly, wondering if he was even asleep. After all, as newlyweds, there was much about each other that we didn't know.

Jeff shouted: "Don't move!"

By the tone of his voice, I pretty quickly decided that: 1) he wasn't sleep-walking; 2) he sounded scared; and 3) there was no way I was going to continue lying still when he was staring at something next to me, something which frightened a grown man.

I shot out of bed in one swift movement, and with my back flush against the wall, I looked where he looked. There, walking ever so nonchalantly over my pillow crawled a very large spider.

"Nice listening," he said.

I kept an eye on the intruder while new hubby went to find tissues with which to kill it.

And, yes, it did take a long time to get back to sleep…between being awakened in a fright at weird behavior and by giant spider, as well as with Jeff shaking the bed with his laughing at my disobedience.

***

After a year in Illinois, we moved to Iowa. My new husband had a habit I didn't have. Before he drank from a cup at the sink, he would always swirl water around the cup to rinse it before refilling it to drink even if clean. I always thought this was a waste of time and water until one night I grabbed my glass by the bathroom sink for a drink. By chance, before filling it and downing the liquid as was my usual habit, I saw by the small nightlight light, sitting in the bottom of the glass, a spider. I had to admit, perhaps maybe my husband's habits made sense after all.

***

Jeff has always been loath to kill spiders inside the house. He figures spiders capture and eat the not-so-nice of God's creatures. Me? They used to give me the shivers, however, I too, was loath to kill spiders or any insects (except for mosquitoes, flies and ticks), for I hated to feel and hear the crush of the poor loathsome critter's body vibrating up through my fingers.

When our boys were young and we lived in New York, a rather large (2-inch) spider had made its way into our one and only bathroom, both Jeff and I refused to kill it for different reasons. So it remained. We called it "Legs." Each time the boys or I entered the bathroom, we'd first look around to spot where our new "pet" was (mostly to make sure it was far enough away to not surprise us with its furry little touches). We'd greet it and then do what we went in there to do, and leave Legs be to do his part of living in our household. Scary enough as it was that we allowed a spider to live in our bathroom, he was a thriving, growing spider. His increasing size meant we had unseen creepy-crawlers lurking there as well. So, we cheered him on.

This relationship worked well for several months. And then we had a babysitter, a teenage girl who announced upon our arrival home at the end of the evening that she had killed this monstrous spider in our bathroom. She was so proud. We were so sad. Yes, even me. I mean, it's not like you can place ads for a houseguest willing to come to eat unwanted creatures in your abode.

Farewell, dear Legs. You were good while you lasted.

***

In South Dakota, I once pulled into our drive to find our next-door neighbor sitting on her front porch steps with her young two daughters, a shoe raised in her hand. The image first brought to mind child abuse, but the girls weren't flinching and the shoe wasn't moving. I went over to ask what was up. Seemed they were waiting for the shiny black widow spider to come out of the crack in their steps. The mom preferred to kill it before letting her kids play in the front yard or through the front door. I left them hunt.

***

Moving to Michigan was interesting because we had never lived in a state where there were so many spiders. Spiders, spiders, everywhere. They are nearly as abundant here as mosquitoes. Because the arachnids are so common, there aren't any interesting tales for me to share. All I know is that in the fall, if you put osage oranges around a room you know which has spiders, they will leave. I'm not sure where they are supposed to leave to, but I've invested in many osage oranges over the years. I also know that the brown recluse spider resides here, especially in wood piles, and that their bites can cause infections and kidney failure. So, beware the brown recluse spider and keep your spider-killing shoe handy.

23

Chapter Five – First time fishing

I married into a fishing and hunting family. Before we were married I felt I had to at least experience fishing, real fishing. Not just the safety-pin-at-the-end-of-the-string fishing. My future father-in-law and future brother-in-law were in a rowboat. Jeff and I fished from a canoe. Jeff figured if I wanted to experience fishing that the first thing I had to do was bait my own hook. To show me how, he took a worm out of the Styrofoam container put it on his fishing hook and cast the line away from the canoe. He passed me the bait container.

After five minutes of shivering every time I saw a crawling worm, I told Jeff if he baited my hook for me the first time that I would do it from then on. He just shook his head.

It took me another couple of minutes to finally grab a worm without getting hysterical each time I dropped it onto the floor of the canoe. Of course, I didn't want to hurt the poor wiggly thing, either, so I pressed the hook ever so gently onto the skin. It wiggled wildly.

Worm skin is tough.

After about five minutes, I discovered another fact: worms also dry out. I'd sprinkle water on it to make it feel better. I chose a second worm, and a third. About twenty minutes after the start of my baiting adventure, Jeff, who was not having the peaceful fishing experience with his girlfriend like he had hoped, finally, silently, put a worm on my hook for me. Sweet soul. I honestly was able to hook the worms myself after that, quickly. I even caught a few fish, with the sad realization that the Carlson Family rule was: "If you catch it, you clean it." (i.e., cut off its head, and slice up the belly, and take out the bones and guts.) Jeff's older brother told me he didn't like the feeling of the wigging fish, either, and gave me the marvelous hint of wearing gloves when I cleaned my fish.

Chapter Six – Turtle Cleanup

In 2011, south-central Michigan was the recipient of the largest inland oil spill in the continental USA to date. It started about fifteen miles from our house. The oil poured into the Kalamazoo River which goes through Battle Creek where we lived. The Kalamazoo River then continues on to Lake Michigan. Jeff and I used to like walking along the river. We'd kayaked the Battle Creek River (yes, I know: redundant name) and had often talked about going down the Kalamazoo, any of the sections, to Lake Michigan. But when the river changed to rainbow-colored and stank of oil, we stayed away. I also knew that just six- to twelve-inches below the river bed, there would remain soaked in oil for years to come, perhaps.

I volunteered to help clean the animals, going through a required evening course on the dangers of raw oil and contact with our skin. We were later trained on site at the cleanup station set aside by the Potawatomi Indian Tribe. We learned how to correctly put on and take off hazmat suits and gloves. We learned how to hold and clean the animals, weighing them both before and after to see how much oil we'd removed.

I really wanted to clean ducks or swans or small mammals, or even frogs. I had no interest in the snakes or salamanders. I got turtles. There were a lot of turtles at the center, probably because they were easiest to catch.

At first, I was tentative holding each animal, especially having to stretch their heads out from the shells so I could clean their necks. but as I heard stories from other volunteers, including waiting until the turtle released its snapping hold on her fingers, I gained confidence.

I now know a lot of information about oil. Mostly, it makes me sad, but because I continue to use plastic items (made from oil), and drive a car (using gasoline and oil), and ride airplanes to travel distances, shouldn't it make me hypocritical to feel sad?

My husband reminds me that I belong in a previous century. I would agree with him if it were not for the medical and dental people of today. Although, I know in the Greco-Roman world, between 500 BC and AD 300, silver production polluted the land and water, rivaling today's pollution. Which century is the best?

Jeff and I went to a dinner party with some neighbors we didn't know well. One woman told us that while she was sunbathing on her dock, she'd seen an alligator in our lake. At first, I laughed at her joke. But, she wasn't joking. She'd seen an alligator.

I tried to logically explain that an alligator in a Michigan lake would probably die because of the cold, but also that if there was such a large creature as she described, other people would have reported it.

Right on cue, a young man who lived across the bay told us he, too, had seen it, and refused to go into the water ever since.

Although I still didn't believe them, neither backed down from their stories.

Two years later, while I was engaged in cleaning oil off turtles, I noticed how this one huge snapping turtle at the oil-cleaning center, with its pointed head, just might be mistaken for an alligator. Might be. Could be. If you looked at it for only a moment before screaming and running away.

Then again, the nearby (thirty miles away) alligator sanctuary have taken in thirty alligators so far from Battle Creek residents alone, whose pets had grown too large for their people-houses. (More about this in the Animal Sanctuaries chapter.)

I'm still skeptical about my neighbor's tale. Turtle or alligator?

The first rodeo I attended was in South Dakota, more than twenty years before we Carlsons moved to the state. Jeff and I were at the end of our seven-week honeymoon, heading back east to Wisconsin. (Sidenote: in SD, the term "back east" refers to the eastern part of SD.) We stopped to camp at Wall. My new husband decided to surprise by taking me for a walk after an early supper. We were north of the Badlands, and there were no parks or prairie hiking trails nearby. I had no idea where we were going.

We crossed the street, walked along a huge fenced-in meadow where people were parking their cars and trucks, and on through the vehicle entrance and to the aluminum stands, about a twenty-minute walk from our tent. It was my first rodeo! Jeff's, too. Nearly every spot was filled.

I was impressed how the animals were dwell-trained and controlled at the reigns of their handlers. The bucking bulls and horses were rather thrilling to watch.

The first most exciting thing to happen there, besides watching all the rodeo events live for the first time, was when one of the bronc horses continued kicking after knocking his rider off. The rider assigned to the horse in the random draw quickly got out of the arena with the help of the rodeo clowns. But the horse kept on bucking. On the fence near the chutes (where the bucking horses and bulls burst into the arena) sat several high school kids. When the horse came near, most of them leapt off in time. One girl did not. She was kicked unconscious with a hoof to the head. An ambulance, on hand for any injured riders, responded immediately and took her away.

A little later the announcer said that the horse was in the pasture kicking cars and pickup trucks and trailers, and if anyone had damage, they were to contact the people in charge of the rodeo.

The show concluded. Prizes awarded. People started filing out of the stands. As soon as Jeff and I exited, we realized we had a big problem. The bucking bronco wasn't the only one set loose in the field with the parked cars. So were all of the other animals that we had just seen tossing riders and threatening their lives in the arena with their horns and hooves.

People dashed to the safety of their vehicles and drove off, leaving wider spaces for the animals to meander. It was quite dark by this time. The only lights came from the immediate vicinity of the arena, from the town across the street, and headlights as they went past us. Jeff and I decided to follow the most common path the cars and pickups took, figuring that the passing vehicles would encourage the animals away. Whenever one car passed and a beast was on the other side of the trail, we jogged next to that car or truck for as long as possible until the next one came by. Sometimes there were long gaps between the cars. By God's providence, we made it back through the exit gate and to our campsite without incident, except for our racing hearts.

Chapter Nine – Deer, Oh, Deer!

I've lived in many places where deer have freely roamed.

My first encounters with deer in the wild were in Wisconsin. I would spot them grazing through the many cornfields. They would jerk their heads up in the woods, then turn with white tails up, dashing away. I breathlessly watched them soar gracefully over fences. They were plentiful. Catching a mother and her fawn in the spring was a joy. But it was at dusk, I discovered, year-round, which was when the animals tended to wander. It was therefore vital to be cautious while driving, keeping doubly alert, watching not simply the road, but also either side for the reflective yellow deer eyes lit by my headlights, and slowing to make sure I could stop before they made sudden dash in front of my killing-machine vehicle.

Here in Michigan, we have three to fifteen of the critters pass through our yard now and again. If I don't actually see them, I'll spot their hoofprints in the snow or mud, or in the spring, nibbled down blossoms, veggies, hostas, etc. Tulip buds are like candy to them. One morning I headed out to work noticing the buds and thinking I would cover them with netting later. When I'd returned home, the buds had been eaten away. And then in the fall—in late October and November, when acorns drop—they stop by in the early night to graze on nuts from our front yard, leaving piles of "raisins."

***

When we lived in the Black Hills of South Dakota, one (and only one) spring we had a herd of about forty white-tailed deer who make their residence in our fenced-in backyard for a time. We were the only people in the neighborhood without a dog, therefore our yard became the Deer Haven of Rest.

One morning, hoping to startle the deer off, I dashed out our door, leapt off our porch, and waved my arms, screaming madly. I expected the animals to show me their white tails and leap over the fence. Instead, they turned their huge heads as one and stared at me. I was surprised that they weren't surprised. Then I realized how vulnerable I'd made myself. Knowing that any one of them could crush my skull with one little kick from a powerful hoof, I turned and did the running. I ran back to the porch waving my arms and screaming, hoping they wouldn't pursue. Each afternoon, long after they'd departed, I'd go out and scoop up the numerous piles of "raisins" and dig them into our garden. That following summer my garden particularly flourished.

***

Before moving to South Dakota, my only wild deer encounters were with the stunningly beautiful white-tailed deer. But there in the Black Hills of South Dakota, also lived a different breed, the mule deer. Instead of graceful, I found them…amusing. Not only are mule deer smaller than white-tailed, but they have these large, Dumbo-sized ears, and they are not in the least timid around people. So, when you

31

come upon a mule deer, or several of them, instead of high-tailing it out of there, they simply turn their heads and stare at you like cows, only mule deer have those big ole ears sticking out to the sides.

***

Thankfully, I've never run into a deer while driving, nor has anyone else in our family. But one time in South Dakota, a deer ran into me.

I was heading to my teaching job in the dark pre-dawn hours, the only car going down a four-lane road in Rapid City. I was in the left lane, traveling about 45 mph when in my peripheral vision I caught eyes immediately outside my driver's window. A deer! One moment it was running perpendicular to and towards the car, inches from my window, the next it had twisted sideways. But the sudden turn didn't stop its forward momentum. The deer slammed its full body against our little Sidekick car, shoving it over the entire right lane and onto the shoulder. I stopped as soon as I could, certain there would be a dead deer in the center of the road, but thankful the side widow hadn't busted. I looked back and about, but the deer had vanished. When I arrived at school I was still shaking. I was surprised I was able to open my door. I checked the side, expecting to see it crushed in. There wasn't a mark. My logical mind has no idea why not. I was thankful to be alive, but shall never forget those huge, wide eyes a mere few inches from my own.

In the fall, we will often drive the hour north of us in Michigan to Ionia State Park. It's a large park, a pretty park, and not used very much especially during the off-times when we visit it.

One fall, Jeff and I were hiking around Sessions Lake, about a ninety-minute walk, when we noticed two deer swimming in the middle of the lake. We've seen hundreds of deer before, but never swimming. What caused them to take the water route v.s. going around through the woods? Perhaps there was a bow-hunter who frightened them. We'd been in the park another time, and walked past a bow-hunter perched high in a tree. It was certainly a possibility since it was bow season. Sessions Lake is no pond. It's more a middle-sized lake. The deer looked like they were struggling in the water. There were a couple of small fishing boats on the far side of the lake. And the only other people around were us, Jeff and me, hiking. We were the closest help the deer had, if needed.

Although struggling, the two deer they were committed to reaching the shore. We didn't want to spook them, but when we realized they would make land fine by themselves we also wanted to get closer if we could. By the time they reached the shore, they were about fifty yards from us. We walked quickly so I could get close enough for a picture. I was successful just as one leapt across the trail in front of us. Priceless.

When we lived in NY, in the late 1980's, we Carlsons took a trip east. We'd reserved a camping spot at Acadia national Park near Bar Harbor, Maine. We arrived near six o'clock in the evening and were informed they were full, even though they did have record of our reservation. We sat there for a while, not knowing what to do or where to go so late in the day, figuring even hotels would be full on this weekend night. The man in the booth finally relented and told us since we did have reservations, we could park any place on the hill next to the campground. We'd be the only ones there. We grabbed it. It was more like a grassy mound.

We set up our tent and tossed in our sleeping bags and pads. With no available picnic table or fire pit, like with the regular reserved sites, we sat on a tarp (our "dining room") and ate a cold meal. We weren't complaining. At least we had a place for the night, and our tent was our familiar bedroom on the ground.

After supper, we went for a walk around the "real" campground area. All of the sites had RVs in them. Big ones. Five or ten of our tents could fit in each RV. Still, we pretty much had the campground to ourselves because no one was outside. By this time, it was dusk and growing darker with every minute, for the new moon was coming the following night. We noticed someone had brought a black cat camping with them. It moved around the door of one of the trailers. A few sites down, we saw the cat with its fluffy tail again, sniffing around another RV. We commented on how quickly it had traveled. Then, a few sites down were two black cats around another RV. Odd. That made us glance around at the other sites. We spotted about a dozen black "cats" in the short distance we could see in the dark. By this time, we figured they weren't household cats at all, but couldn't imagine what.

Jeff pulled out his flashlight and shined the light at them. You know the expression "ignorance is bliss?" Yeah. I wish Jeff hadn't pulled out his light, for there in the light beam, it was easy to tell that each animal had a white stripe down its back. Skunks. As we trotted back towards the safety of our tent, we noticed skunks around nearly every RV. We sprinted the rest of the way back.

By the time we arrived at our hill, we found we had neighbors. No, not skunks.

There were several vehicles now parked on the top of the mound with several tents getting set up in a circle. There were men, women, and teens, about twenty people in all. They'd started a bonfire, a fire without fire pit or grate limiting the size of flames. Spanish music blared from their "site."

The amount of company, the noise, those were surprises. But there was also a man chopping wood about thirty feet from our tent. He welded a machete.

Throughout the night, I watched their bonfired silhouettes dancing over our tent walls, wondering if we'd be "mistaken" in the night for firewood, or if their unattended fire would sweep down the mound to us. Perhaps the skunks would be our heroes and drive them into their tents and RVs. None of those happened. It was a long night.

In the morning, we Carlsons were packed and gone before any, I mean, *any*, of our neighbors awakened.

Chapter Twelve – SD Fletcher

In spring of the late 1990s, while living in Rapid City, SD, Jeff and I were awakened for the second day in a row by a fletcher (woodpecker) pecking on our roof. It's bad enough being rat-a-tat-tatted at five AM, but the fact that the bird is doing this seemed to indicate that our roof has bugs! The boys couldn't hear it because the bird was making its racket above our bedroom, about four feet to the slanted roof and just above our headboard. Our roof peaked and then slanted the other way down to John's room. Peter's room was below John's, so they both slept soundly through it all.

I went out five times in the early morning to shoo it away, waving my arms and then a towel. It flew to the tree a few feet away, sitting there watching me until I went back inside and climbed back into the bed before it started its pecking once more.

The following morning, we went into the garage at five AM and dug out Jeff's old Super Soaker. I put a teaspoon of dish soap in it, hoping to discourage any bugs as well as scare away the bird.

Jeff got dressed and went out to the deck. As soon as he went out the door, the bird flew to the tree and sat there looking at him. Jeff aimed to spray the soap water up on the roof when from behind him, on the other side of the fence, only a few feet away, a mule deer suddenly panicked at his arrival, and bolted down our backyard.

Jeff returned to bed telling me it was my turn the next time the bird rat-a-tat-tatted.

It didn't take long. About thirty minutes later I was on the deck in my robe and slippers and not-brushed-hair. I had Jeff's Super Soaker in hand. The bird was not in its normal corner of the house above our bed. The sound now came from the front of the house, above John's room.

I went out our front wooden gate and stood in the daylight of early morn in my robe and slippers and messed up hair. I soaked the corner of the roof where the bird was.

Thing is, people in that Rapid City neighborhood tended to take walks very early in the morning. The newspaper also arrived by 6 or 6:15 each day. I didn't care. I had an issue with that bird.

Later I discovered fletchers don't peck for insects in gutters. This was a male bird trying to attract female birds with his very loud pecking. Apparently, the louder the noise, the more appealing he is. Pecking on a metal roof gutter makes for a much louder sound than on a wooden tree. Much. Louder.

The following year, Mr. Fletcher returned. He pecked at our

gutter and was oblivious to our Super Soaker warnings. That year he attracted three females who nested in three different trees in our backyard. I guess his loud gutter-pecking worked.

Chapter Thirteen – Pitbulls and Puppies

When I was 19- and 20-years-old, I was involved in Volunteers in Service to America (aka, V.I.S.T.A.), today renamed AmeriCorps. My assignment was to work with senior citizens in the Bottoms of Des Moines, Iowa. This area of town was called the Bottoms because it was adjacent to the Des Moines River and lay even lower than the levied river, so sometimes flooded like a river bottom. There were only two paved road through there in the late 1960's, only a couple of miles from the gold-domed state capital building. 50% of the houses in the Bottoms did not have indoor plumbing. And only 10% of the houses had indoor toilets. I was given the vague task of finding seniors, ascertaining their needs, and meeting those.

One day, I went to check on an elderly single lady another had recommended I visit. I found her house and parked the government car on the side dirt road next to the front of the house. Halfway to the porch, more bent on my new V.I.S.T.A. contact than on my environment, I noticed movement. About fifteen feet away, a pitbull stalked me, inching closer and closer. As soon as I saw it (or rather, as soon as he saw I saw him), he began growling and snarling and moving closer to me faster. I was too far from the car to run to it without getting latched onto by dog teeth. I froze. He continued.

I took a step backwards. The bulldog took two steps towards me. He was closing the gap faster than I could back up. When the dog was about six feet from me, a woman came out of the house next door and called to the dog by name. The dog stopped moving but kept growling and snarling without taking his eyes off of me. Even then, when I took a step backward, the dog approached a step forward. The neighbor asked what I was doing there. I explained I wanted to check on her neighbor, that I was a V.I.S.T.A. volunteer, a familiar name in that neighborhood.

I remained still while the neighbor walked over and took a hold of the dog's collar. She said she was watching the dog for her neighbor who was gone for a few days, but that she felt too sorry for the poor thing tied up on his leash all day that she just let him wander free.

The day after the pitbull incident, I went to check on a friendly elderly couple I knew from numerous visits to their house. As I stepped on the porch I spied a puppy tied by a length of rope around his neck and to the porch railing. At the sight of me, it backed itself into the corner, so scared it peeed on the porch. I soon found out that the couple had gotten the puppy only the day before. I wondered how such a young thing could be so scared. I could only assume it had been abused earlier in its short life.

The irrational thing about this was my reaction. I had never been afraid of dogs, but as a result of my previous day's visit elsewhere, I found myself suddenly scared of anything "dog," and surprised to find that I was as terrified of this pup as he was of me. I'm only thankful that I, too, didn't pee on the porch.

***

Decades later, in Michigan, we lived in a residential neighborhood with narrow streets and no sidewalks. It was a normally quiet place to take walks. I went down a neighboring street that I had not walked down before. Suddenly, an unleashed bulldog charged at me from a front porch. The yard was not fenced in. Nor was there a silent electric fence sign in the yard. Normally, I would have been terrified, especially after a previous bulldog charge. Instead, I began laughing. For in its mouth, was a stuffed teddy bear. It seemed silly to be frightened of such a cute little dog carrying around his stuffed toy, even if he might have dropped the teddy bear to rip my limbs off.

The owner called him back, assuring me that he would not have hurt me. I would have to wait for another day to be terrified.

Another neighbor owned a Rottweiler. They have a fenced-in back yard, but the dog was often in the front, chasing down cyclists, or walkers who quickly became runners. I knew the dog's name because the owners called to him so often. I could watch his antics from my backyard. He liked to bark at the lawnmower when the owner mowed the grass. So…it was natural for him to do the same with me when he'd wander into my yard when I mowed. Unlike his owner, I didn't trust the animal would move out of harm's way when the spinning blades came near, so when he got too close, I'd stop moving. The dog stopped barking and looked up at me. I started forward. The dog hunched down into barking-attack-mode until it came within inches of the machine again and I'd stop. It was a fun game, even though it took longer to mow the yard when the neighbor dog "helped."

Chapter Fourteen – Carlson-Stark Pets

Before she married my dad, my mother spent some time in Florida. She stayed in a room of a house of an elderly woman. One day before leaving for work. Mom found a tarantula in her room. She killed it and tossed it in the garbage. When she returned home from work, her landlady was visibly upset. All day long, she had searched the house for her pet tarantula. Mom rushed to a pet store, bought another one without telling her, set it loose in the house, and the next day found another place to live.

***

My mother was raised on a farm and always had animals both inside and outside the house (but not pet spiders). After she'd had two children, she wanted to have a dog to round out her family. I don't even know the name of it since I was an infant when this happened. All I know is that the puppy was black, and it didn't stay with us long. Mom returned the dog because she became annoyed of both changing my diapers and of cleaning up after the dog. I guess the dog was easier (and more legal) to get rid of than me.

***

When I was eleven, my brother saw what he thought was a raccoon go into my grandparents' barn. He chased after it to find it wasn't a raccoon at all, but a kitten with a raccoon tail. We begged, like we did on every visit to the farm, if we could keep it. To our utter surprise, the parents agreed.

Roger named our cat Spice because besides the raccoon tail, he had salt and pepper markings. I always considered Spice my cat since he spent most of the daytime in my room. However, as a grown up I realize it was probably because I had the sunniest room of the house.

When I was sixteen, Spice became very, very sick, not eating and hardly moving. He wouldn't let Mom come near him (scratching/hissing) to take him to the vet. So, she asked me to get him into the travel box. I called to him from the kitchen landing. He came, but cried out in pain every one of the seven steps up to me. I gently picked him up—he meowed pitifully enough to make me cry—and I placed him in the box.

When I got home from school, I immediately asked Mom about Spice. After all, he was "my" cat. I was worried all day for him.

She answered to look on the desk in my room. I thought that was a peculiar place to leave Spice, and how did she keep him there? But Spice was not there. On the desk was a note in Mom's handwriting, written on the back of a used envelope: "Spice had a kidney infection. We had to put him down."

My mother was never very good dealing with death, which seems strange for a farm girl. We never discussed it further. I was very sad.

***

In the late 1950's, we Stark kids traded a deck of tiny playing cards for a baby turtle that a neighbor had caught near Devil's Lake, Michigan. We took it home to Ohio and had it for a few years in a plastic container in the breakfast area. Mom loved that little turtle, who always watched her each time she passed. We named him Oscar. After a couple of years, she decided our little turtle needed a friend, so the following August, back at the lake, we got another baby turtle we called Clam. Who knew baby turtles could be so adorable? We had them for two years when we were leaving on a family trip for a week. Mom thought it would be good experience to pass the turtles next-door, for the six-year-old boy, Bobby, to take care of and teach him some responsibility. I'm not sure what his official diagnosis would be today but he was hyperactive, threw tantrums, and was mean to everybody in the neighborhood. When we got back from our vacation, Mom rushed next door to get her turtles back. She returned looking like she was going to throw up. The first day our pets were in his care, Bobby flushed Oscar and Clam down the toilet.

***

While in college, my brother had a pet skunk he named I. Ode Fenwick III. He was de-clawed, and obviously de-scented (the skunk, not by brother). I. Ode was cute, and Roger cuddled it, but I would never hold it because 1) it was a skunk, and 2) when it got angry, it stood up on his hind legs, opened his mouth, and rapidly swung his arms in a blur like a fast-moving windmill.

***

My sister and husband have had dogs. My brother and wife have had dogs. Jeff's brother had dogs. Jeff's sister had dogs. Our one son has two cats. The other son has a dog and two African tortoises. My husband has always said he would allow me to have a dog when he died. His exact words: "Over my dead body." That said, it did not prevent us Carlsons from having pets.

I knew that Jeff would give hesitation with us having large mammals, like dogs or cats, but when he was gone to California for two weeks for a Fuller Seminary course, the boys and I got ourselves a fish tank along with some goldfish. What argument could there be with fish? They didn't shed. They were out of the way, and easy to care for. Then I read about goldfish—some living for seventy years! I wondered who we could will our fish to. Of course, over the course of the first three days, most of the fish died. But there was one who survived. He'd turned color from golden-orange to solid white. I don't

44

remember the original name we gave him, but after his resurrection and color change, we renamed him Gandalf, after the White Wizard. We waited to make sure he survived and then got him a companion. Jeff named this fish. He called him Andy—an acronym for And Not Dead Yet. He lived for several years.

The one and only time we four Carlsons went on a three-week vacation, we went camping (of course). When we returned, I realized to my horror that the month-long fish food cube was sitting on the edge of the aquarium. I'd left it for the last thing to do before we left the house and then forgot it. Three weeks without food, and still our two fish lived. They were living, but mad.

For nearly a week, whenever I passed the aquarium, they each positioned their faces in the far corner of the tank, as if turning their backs on me in revenge for me turning my back on them. I'd tap the three soft taps on the lid before feeding them, as I normally did. These taps used to bring them open-mouthed to the surface. Not during this time. It took them nearly a month of punishing me before they forgave me and finally returned to the surface at my light tap.

Until this incident, I never knew fish could have feelings or personalities. Surprise!

***

Another time Jeff went to a seminary class, fourth-grader John got a golden hamster. John liked the sound of the nocturnal creature running on the wheel in his bedroom because, "He keeps away robbers at night."

In New York, we also got a gerbil (Peter's), a hermit crab (John's), and two sibling dwarf hamsters (John's), who then started having babies after a month. We "lost" our two old goldfish when it became very hot for several days and they leapt right out of the warmed aquarium water through the small opening in the tank lid. I felt awful. I didn't realize the water had gotten so warm!

When we moved to South Dakota, we gave away all our Carlson pets.

Chapter Fifteen – My Pet Rabbit

Riding home from a morning college class, I noticed a slight movement in a wooded lot. Curious, I climbed off my bike to discover a baby rabbit. A wild baby rabbit that wasn't frightened of me. I looked around to find its mama or siblings. No one. I'd seen a large cat stalking these woods, so perhaps the bunny was an orphan. I decided to save it from Fat Cat. I grabbed a piece of litter (a paper cup), placed the cute little thing inside, and took it back to my apartment. I placed it in a shoe box with grass for bedding, lettuce for eating, and water for drinking, then put a screen over the top with a weight.

By late afternoon, the poor little thing still hadn't moved, not even to nibble on the lettuce leaf. I put it in its traveling cup and made my only-ever visit to a vet.

"What's wrong with it?"

"It's wild. You need to set it free."

"But what's wrong with it? Why won't it eat?"

"It's scared. It's wild. You need to set it free."

The compassionate vet didn't charge me for my visit. I was too sad to care one way or the other. I decided to keep it, anyway. It was so cute and helpless. It was my pet, and the little darling needed me. That was what I decided, that is, until nighttime.

All night long, that tiny, helpless critter kept me awake as it thrashed and crashed against the box and the screen. It had turned into Bunnicula.

The next morning, I got it back into its travelling cup and rode to the woods where I'd found it. I set the cup down near the spot and left some lettuce, in case it needed some energy after its night terrors. It didn't dart from the cup. I stepped back to the road and watched for a while. Still no movement. I wished it well, prayed for Fat Cat to keep away, and left.

I waited one long day before I checked on it. The cup was still there. The rabbit was not.

Later I realized that when I found it, it was probably either injured or too scared to move. Obviously, he was cured, and had found his family…or perhaps eaten. But it was wild. It belonged in the wild. I'm sure I did what was best by setting it free. Didn't I?

Chapter Sixteen – LuLu the Elephant

In 1986, we moved through a two-day blizzard in two cars from Iowa to New York with a toddler and a preschooler. A person from our new church gave us a one-year family membership to the Buffalo Zoo—the third oldest zoo in the USA. After that first gifted year, we purchased family membership passes for the following nine years, until we left New York state.

Elephants have always fascinated me. I could write a book or three with all the information I have on the animals. But there was one particular elephant I met there in New York: Her name was LuLu.

It's true that elephants have good memories. I know from both reading and personal experience. Each time I'd visit the zoo, I stopped first by the elephant enclosure, calling out to LuLu. She'd come to the fence and reach out her trunk towards me, just beyond my outstretched arm. The other elephants remained where they were, but not my friend. I'd quietly sing to LuLu, while my boys and husband scurried away from The Crazy Lady singing to the elephants, as they rushed towards the more interesting and quieter polar bears.

A few years later, LuLu became even more special to me when

I discovered we were born the same year. When I visited the zoo each year on my own birthday month, I'd sing "Happy birthday to us."

This story does not have a happy ending. LuLu died of an abscessed tooth when she was in her 40's. In the 19th century, this was the leading cause of death for people. We now know how to prevent that from happening—to people. But by the time the elephant keepers figured out why LuLu wasn't eating, the infection had spread too far.

As she lay dying in the enclosed elephant house, knowing how family-oriented elephants are, the keepers decided to bring in the other elephants huddled at the door. They gathered around LuLu and rubbed their trunks tenderly over her large grey body. I wish I could have been there, too, touching her, being with her, singing to her, there at the very end of her life. Good-bye, LuLu, my friend.

Chapter Seventeen – Creatures in a Rowboat

When I was twelve-years-old, I earned five dollars a week as a junior counselor at Shaker Day Camp in Hudson, Ohio. I was assigned to the 5- and 6-year-old campers.

One sunny summer day, I took five of the kids with me out in a rowboat. None of us had on life preservers. There wasn't even one in the boat. It wasn't a law back then, plus at the little kids' end of the lake it was shallow enough to stand in the two feet of water. Of course, heavier teens and adults would have sunk about knee-deep in the muck.

So here I was, a kid myself, rowing the younger kids through the lake shallows. I decided to stop at one of the grassy tree stumps sticking up out of the water. I clasped onto the grass as we sat unmoving in the water. Someone had joined us at our stump stop: a very plump spider which crawled around the flat bottom of the rowboat.

Not wanting to frighten the kids, I took one of the oars from the oar lock and proceeded to crush the spider. I was never very good at killing even bugs, or arachnids—I hated killing anything—so it was a reluctant, slow crush, ending with a "pop." Suddenly—to my horror—hundreds of itsy bitsy baby arachnids covered the floor of the boat. They were everywhere, climbing up the sides of the boat, climbing over the oars. The plump spider I'd murdered had, of course, been pregnant.

I calmly put the oar back into the lock, and rowed back to shore in about one tenth of the time it had taken me to reach the stump.

Chapter Eighteen – Roosters

I was raised in a suburb of a large city, but down on my grandparents' farm, getting awakened by the call of a rooster was all a part of the farming experience. It sounded right, natural and homey. Being greeted each morning by a rooster is the perfect alarm clock for waking up on a farm.

The chicken coop was the closest building to the farm house. I imagine it was built there to make it easier to collect eggs, but it was also easier, if you were not paying attention, to step in chicken poop when using the back door.

***

The family story goes that when my father was dating my mother, Granddad decided that my dad needed to kill a chicken for supper. Granddad did not supervise. He just let his future son-in-law prove his manhood by going out and providing supper. I'm sure Dad was egotistical and proud enough to respond something similar to, "No problem."

Apparently, Dad did have a problem. Chase as he might, he could not catch any of the chickens. They were lightning fast. However, there was one particular skinny chicken who kept following him around. It was rather scrawny, but having failed to catch one of the plump ones, Dad figured it was the only one he could get, and chicken was chicken. He grabbed it, chopped off its head on the wooden stump, and brought the dead fowl inside.

Turns out, this particular one wasn't one of the plentiful hens from the coop at all. It was Granddad's pet rooster, the pet who greeted him at the backdoor, and followed him all around the farmyard.

***

One time down on the farm, we three free-ranging kids found an egg in one of the out buildings. It was a good distance from the coop, and rather hidden behind rusted tools. Big Brother Roger thought it would be fun to smash that lone, forgotten egg. He wisely took it outside so the mess would be contained in the yard and not inside the building. He grabbed a hammer and gave that old egg a tap. Did I mention old? I'm not sure its exactly age, but from the putrid smell which penetrated the air, I'm guessing centuries. We ran, screaming, towards the farmhouse, desperately gasping for fresh air.

***

While on a mission trip to Tijuana, Mexico, I worked at Casa de la Esperanza Orfanato for two weeks. The people who ran the orphanage were very organized and fairly self-sufficient.

They had chickens, lots and lots of chickens. We had scrambled eggs every morning for breakfast, and if there were leftovers they were reheated for lunch.

There was also a rooster in the flock. We Americanos on the trip stayed in a building closest to the chicken coop. The result being every morning, starting at 3:30 AM, the rooster would begin crowing. It was still dark at that time, of course. Then it crowed every seven seconds. I even recorded it for proof. Every. Seven. Seconds. I found myself relating to my dad's action a few decades earlier of killing the rooster, but with an entirely different motive in mind.

Cock-a-doodle-doo!

Sadly, we three spoiled city kids refused to drink the warm milk from the cows right there on my grandparents' farm. We had to have the homogenized and purified city-milk. Fresh milk tasted yucky.

Once I watched Granddad milk a cow. Usually we kids had to be out of sound and sight from the regular farm activities. Granddad sat on a low three-legged stool in the barn at the milking end of the cow. Barn cats suddenly surrounded him. I can still hear his chuckle as he squirted milk into the mouths of those kittens.

***

We'd go into the barn, climbing and sliding around on the bales of hay. We did that lots until one time Mom came looking for us and found us playing in the hay loft. She told us it was dangerous. But since we'd been doing it for years, we obviously questioned why. We could fall. Well, that never happened except for soft landings on more hay. She told us we could get trapped between the bales. Again, never happened. She told us there were snakes and rats which hid in the cracks between the bales. We three were out of the barn before Mom finished her sentence, and never played there again.

***

When I was just out of sixth grade, Granddad and Dad and Roger took a fishing trip to Canada for a week. Mom, Bette, and I stayed down on the farm with Grandmother. After lots of begging from me to help with do farm chores, Grandmother finally gave me one, and only one job: collect the eggs from inside the henhouse. I'd never been inside the out-of-bounds henhouse. It was stinky. Always. And to get to it, you had to do some tricky footwork so as not to step in any chicken poop.

So, I was able to do my farm chore at last. It was late morning, and most of the hens were outside the house. Most. There was one who sat on her nest, glaring at me as I entered. A chicken giving a ten-year-old city slicker the evil eye can be a bit unnerving. I tried to chase her out, but she had none of it. I didn't collect any egg she may or may not have been sitting on. How did Grandmother know? I confessed I skipped that one. She took me out with her, brushed the chicken off the nest, and collected the egg. The following mornings, I was confident enough to do it by myself, and was successful.

***

My brother Roger was allowed to shoot guns on the farm. My sister and I were never allowed this activity. Girls weren't "permitted" to do things like that. But we could follow "the boy" around to see what he did, alone on the farm with gun slung over his shoulder. There were no hunter training courses back then.

54

Once, Roger decided to shoot a snake he spotted on a log near one of the barns. (Yes, I know. Foolish unsupervised children with guns.) He shot it on the first try. We ran over to see the result. Hundreds of writhing baby snakes from the burst body of the mama snake, and three screaming kids ran back to the safety of the farmhouse.

***

On summer evenings, the adults pulled dining room chairs out to in front of the porch. Adults sat in the chairs while we kids ran around catching fireflies. We put them in jars with grass we'd pulled up to feed them and keep them happy. We poked holes in the metal lids with ice picks and left them on the dressers next to us as we slept to use as night lights.

In the morning, every single time, those poor insects had died, and the jars smelled of firefly death. We kept doing it for several years because fireflies are cool, and we were always hopeful to release them in the morning…alive.

***

There was the time before the house was built on the hill above the farmhouse that we would spend many an afternoon lying on that hilltop, gazing at the sky and playing the cloud game. "I see an elephant." "There is a dragon head." "I see a bird." This was a cherished place to be, until one year I looked next to me to find the shed skin of a blue racer (snake). The next year, the house was built, so snakes or not, cloud-watching from that hill was now forbidden.

There is the family story of the time when Great Aunt Jess was out at the cottage to open it up for the summer. At night, she went up to her normal bedroom. After she had crawled in, she felt movement near her feet. When she pulled back the covers there at the base of the bed between the sheets she discovered a mouse had made a nest, including several mice.

That was the same room and same bed I slept in. Even though I dreamed of mice at my feet, there were none in reality.

***

Another cottage pastime was standing at the end of the dock and feeding minnows the end pieces of bread.

When I was a teen, I thought it would be grand to get the minnows closer to me. I took several slices of bread, and while in my swimming suit, knelt up to my chest in the water. I started sprinkling crumbs around me, calling out to the little fishies to "come and get it."

At first, no one came. Then two arrived. Then six. Soon I was surrounded with dozens of teeny minnows wanting bread. I couldn't feed them fast enough, and soon nearly ran out of bread. Did that fact deter those little fish? Nope. Soon they started nibbling on me! On my arms, my legs, my chest, my back. I had gathered around me my own

Devil's Lake piranha eating away at me. I stood and splashed to shore, screaming and flailing my arms the entire way.

***

There were also fireflies lighting up the neighborhood at dusk. My brother and sister and I loved catching them down on our grandparents' farm. So, we joined in the summer chase with the other cottage kids. To my horror, one of the boys started making jewelry for us girls. He'd capture a firefly, wait for it to light up, then snap it in half to keep the tail lit after its death. He'd then use the lit bug guts to stick onto fingers or necks or put in our hair. EW!!!

Chapter Twenty-one – Bird and Animal Sanctuaries

There are wild animals and birds all over the world. They can be found in neighborhoods and parks and wilderness areas. There are also designated sanctuaries. We've driven and hiked through many bird sanctuaries in various states, marsh or lake land set aside mainly for migrating birds.

In Michigan—the state which started the first Audubon Society, one year before the national one began—I've attended events at a couple of sanctuaries: the Sandhill Crane Festival at the Bernard W. Barker Sanctuary near Bellevue, and a star-watch at the Kellogg Bird Sanctuary near Augusta, where I also identified evening bird calls in the dark. Jeff and I have also hiked around the Haehnle Bird

Sanctuary near Pleasant Lake. At Yankee Springs Recreation Area near Hastings, there is a sign near the beach area which reads: "Geese Natural Habitat. Watch your step. Please do not feed." I find this sign amusing, since Canada geese are everywhere in Michigan, year-round. My guess is that anywhere near any lake is their natural habitat.

Also in Michigan, we have the Critchlow Alligator Sanctuary near Athens, where they've taken in hundreds of no-longer-wanted reptiles. It's the only Alligator Sanctuary within nine hundred miles, and thirty of their alligators came from Battle Creek! They actually train some of their alligators who learn to come when they hear their names called, able to distinguish the difference between Ned and Ted. An alligator named Grace had her hand bit off by another alligator at a previous location. Whenever they want to examine her, every ninety days or so, they don't jump on her back or flip her over or sedate her. Instead, they call her over to them by name. At their command, she raises her arm with the missing hand for the five- to nine-second time needed to examine it. What is this command? "Fist bump." Each October, Critchlow's has an Alligator Roundup to take the animals into buildings for the winter. Safely inside, they do not eat again until spring.

In Western New York, our sons' Cub Scout troop went to a private Environmental Refuge, where they took in about a dozen wolves and several birds, mostly which had been so injured by cars they were unable to be released into the wild. Both boys held huge birds on their arms. Very cool.

Our first Carlson house was situated on the edge of Fort Dodge, Iowa. The other side of our fence was a corn field one year followed in rotation by soybeans the next. Sadly, people with unwanted pets from town would drop them off in the country. From there the animals wandered back towards civilization, where I'd call the animal catcher. We couldn't keep them, but I didn't want to think about what happened to the little critters after they left us.

***

A couple years before that, while engaged to Jeff, we headed into the farmland west of busy Dubuque, Iowa. There was no GPS for public back then, so we explored on our own, turning down whichever gravel or dirt road looked interesting. We figured we'd find our way back to an east-west road sometime by noticing sun direction. Deep within the twistings and turnings, we spotted a sign indicating a county park, so followed it to the top of a hill. We parked, walked about, looking out over the scenic rural Iowa countryside.

We returned to the car, climbed in, and started a few yards down the hill when a pack of twenty wild dogs charged over that hill and surrounded our car, growling, barking, and jumping on our vehicle. The thought occurred to us both that if we had remained on that hilltop, outside our car, for even two minutes longer, they would have killed us. We drove along the dusty dirt road at about 25 mph, safe within our car, but with the pack keeping up with us. After a couple miles, only the lead dog remained with us, but at last even he gave up.

We passed a farmhouse with barn and outbuildings while Jeff and I reflected on being minutes away from being torn and eaten alive. We heard shouting and gun shots. We wondered how many of the dogs the farmer had killed or scared off, but prayed both he and his animals were safe.

Chapter Twenty-three – More Dogs, Unleashed

There was also the time in Algonquin Provincial Park in Ontario, Canada, where we four Carlsons hiked Lookout Trail. The rule of the park was that all dogs had to be on six-foot leashes. About half of all the dog-owner visitors we met there followed the rule.

Seven-year-old John decided that he wanted to lead the hike. We always stayed close on hikes, so we parental units didn't think it would be dangerous to let the youngest lead.

As John crested a hill, a large black animal charged him, first running silently, then growling, and then barking with bared teeth.

It was a dog, a dog nearly the size of John. He later confessed that he thought for sure the big and black animal was a bear.

The owners of the dog hiked about fifty yards behind. We four froze while the dog kept us at bay with his growling until his owners caught up to him, laughing at us being so scared of their gentle dog. Besides breaking park rules and terrorizing children (and adults), I imagine this group with their loose dog were unable to see much wildlife during their stay in the wilds of Algonquin.

***

When Jeff was in high school in the late 1960s he was cross country training alone in Wisconsin Dells when a large dog spotted him. It started chasing him. It was so big, he thought it might've been a Great Dane. The distance was far enough away that Jeff was able to get away.

***

Fall of my freshman year in college, I took the required speech class. For every speech that semester, I'd received an A (perfect) along with praise from the professor. I got more praise than she'd given any other student. The final speech was to be a persuasive speech. She stressed that it needed to be controversial. Apparently, I chose too controversial a topic, one with which the professor obviously didn't agree. For that final speech grade, she gave me an F (fail).

This unfair bias confused me. I didn't even support the topic I'd chosen to defend. I'd taken up the challenge and was going for controversy. Succeeded.

By evening, I was not just confused, but depressed. I needed to be alone. If professors had that much power, I wanted to drop out of college. I walked alone down rural roads with no streetlights.

Cleared corn fields lay on either side of the road except for the occasional farm house.

From one of the houses a Doberman rushed at me from behind and bit me on my butt. I was wearing a heavy winter coat so the dog had grabbed only cloth. I was too depressed to be scared, so dragged the growling dog with me as I walked pitifully on. The dog finally listened to his owner shouting from the house and reluctantly let me go.

***

In the early 1970s when I was teaching in Baraboo, Wisconsin, I went cross-country skiing alone on frozen Lake Delton, just a few miles north of where I lived. The temperature was quite chilly, but the sky bright blue and the snow twinkling white as I broke a trail through it. The wooded hills surrounding the lake felt like a natural hug. It was all so stunningly beautiful that I stopped in the middle of the lake. With my ski pole, I made a circle in the snow around my skis and me, and stood there praising God for all this beauty.

Then, from across the lake, I noticed five dogs had come from the hills onto the lake. They lopped towards me. I knew I couldn't outrun them (rather, outski them), so I stayed where I was and watched the pack of five as they surrounded me. By this time, there was no direction I could go, plus I had skis strapped to my shoes limiting my movement. The dogs growled and inched their way closer.

All I could think of for defense was that I could probably use the metal tip of my poles to injure one or two of them, but knew that would only incite the rest. When they were just five feet from me, already inching into my snow-marked circle, someone unseen from the far shore started yelling at them to "come." It took about five minutes of that person shouting before the dogs finally turned and left me. I decided that time alone in God's glorious creation, with wood strips strapped to my shoes, had concluded for the day. I turned around and retraced my trail back to my car.

***

In Michigan, in the 2000-teens, Jeff and I would go to Michigan's West Coast to walk the sand beaches, in fall, winter, or spring—times when they weren't crowded. However, now and again we'd come across dog owners with their dogs unleashed, even though there were signs near the beach reading, "No Dogs Allowed on the Beach." Once, I pointed out the sign to a man as he was passing it while his dog sniffed and pawed at us. The owner commented, "Oh, I know. We only come here during off season." Too bad dogs can't read. They'd probably be obedient about following rules.

When Peter was four months old, we took him camping for the first time, in April, at Kettle Moraine State Park in Wisconsin. It was cold enough that weekend for us to wear our down jackets during the day. In the morning, Jeff broke the ice off the top layer of our water container so it would pour out. That night, Peter slept beside me inside my old down coat, the perfect sleeping bag size for a four-month-old. However, he cried out several times in the night. My guess was because of the unusual setting. Each time, I sat cross-legged on my sleeping bag and nursed him—that warm little body at my chest whom I longed to wrap my freezing-cold hands around! Thankfully for him, protective mommy mode prevailed.

We were the only ones in the campground that weekend. In fact, we were the only ones in the entire state park. Human, that is.

The men's one-holer outhouse was not far from our site, and close to the water pump. To reach the women's outhouse, I had to pass the men's and then travel about fifty yards through a small woods to an open area where other campsites were. All empty. I liked the walk alone through the woods. It was a nice break. Except at dusk.

As I walked there, away from the warm fire and into the black woods—oh, and I almost never carry a flashlight because it makes everything around me look even darker except in that tiny circle of light at my feet—I heard a great whooshing sound, followed by the flap of wings. I'm assuming a great horned owl swooped close enough to my head that I felt the rush of wind as it passed.

I ran the rest of the way to the outhouse and did what I went to do. On my way back, I took off my coat and swung it in circles about my head. The smart owl didn't dive at me again. From then on, I used the men's outhouse. It was one of those rare times that I wished I had a flashlight so I could have identified exactly what sort of creature it was. Again, I'm only assuming it was an owl.

Chapter Twenty-five – Chatter Around the Pup

Jeff and I were less than a year married when we decided to backpack to a secluded campsite in Door County, Wisconsin. It was early spring. No mosquitoes. No other campers. Just us and nature next to Lake Michigan. How romantic.

Because we had backpacked in, we naturally took our two-person nylon pup tent. For two skinny adults to lay down in it meant lying on our sides or on our backs with one elbow on your partner's tummy and the other pushing out against the tent. But we were newlyweds. We were alone. How romantic.

We'd stayed outside by our campfire burning in the designated firepit trying to get warm, turning this way and that toward the fire until it was quite black out there in the woods by the lakeshore. At last we put out the fire and crawled into our tent and sleeping bags, bumping into each other a dozen times taking off our shoes and putting them outside the door, and finally wiggling to prone positions.

We hadn't yet fallen asleep when we heard an unidentified noise, and later felt…something.

The noise was a chattering. Like cold teeth pounding together, only about fifty times faster, and loud. It was as if the entire forest were listening, too, for there were no other animal or bird noises. It—whatever it was—kept its distance, about twenty feet from our tiny tent, and about ten feet high.

As Sasquatch and visions from teen horror movies flashed through my mind, I carefully patted in my jeans' pocket for my pocket knife. I know-know-know that you're never supposed to use a weapon which can be taken away and used against you. Knowledge didn't matter, except that we couldn't identify what made the chattering sound. We didn't dare move around in our tent to look out to see. If my wilderness husband was concerned. We both lay silent and motionless, both pretending to be asleep, but both wide awake.

The sound came from lower and lower until it was on ground level with us. Whatever it was crept and stalked near the ground, each step taking a full second or two.

The only way I could be closer to my husband would be if I lay on top of him, or under him.t I was too petrified to move.

It chattered at our tent door. I lifted my head and waited for it to unzip the pup tent and slash us up and eat us. It didn't.

Instead, it moved to my left, across my feet area at the door. And then slowly, all the while *chit-chit-chitt*-ing, worked its way along the side of the tent, scraping against it, pushing it in, as if at any moment it would rip that nylon as it headed up toward my face. I could feel as well as hear exactly where it was. I gripped my pocket knife tighter.

Whatever it was went the full perimeter of our tent.

Then the night was silent.

Jeff and I did not speak. We did not move. I finally fell asleep with my pocket knife clutched in my fist near my neck, ready to open and use at any moment's notice.

In the morning, we looked for traces of what had happened. Nothing. No footprints. No drag marks. Nothing.

Later that day as we hiked the woods, we were caught in a tornado. We ran back to our car and showed up early at some friends' house. Mel was a ranger that year. Jeff and I were both soaking wet, hoping to dry our clothes. Our friends didn't have a washer or drier. They washed up at the laundromat in town. We stripped and put on their robes while our clothes dried by their fireplace. We told Mel our story.

"Sounds like a porcupine," he said.

He grew up in Door County. He must know these things. But to this day I have my doubts about what creature made the chit-chit-chattering and scraping the sides of our tent in the dead of night.

In the late 1980's, we four Carlsons took a family camping trip around our new state of New York. The boys were three- and six-years-old. One of the nights we stayed at Cranberry Lake near Saranac.

We'd been traveling longer than normal that day and it was already evening when we drove around the very full camp area. We pulled into the only available site left. It was right across the campground road from what looked like a barrel dumpster on its side. We didn't think much about it at the time. We were just glad to have a place to lay our heads for the night.

We first put up the tent and then made a quick supper. We had a campfire, but that night, since it was late and time for little boys to be in their sleeping bags, we didn't sit around it long.

Our normal camping routine at bedtime was for me to get the boys settled in the tent and then I'd join Jeff by the campfire for half an hour or more of adult time. But this night, while inside the nylon tent with the boys, I noticed headlights moving slowly past our campsite, then completely stop. I called out to Jeff to see ask what was up. He responded he didn't know. I watched and waited, then Jeff's shadow as he rose from the campfire area and walk past our tent in the direction of the car still stopped in front of our site.

He was silent. The car hadn't moved.

Several minutes passed until I finally shouted out, "Everything okay?"

He didn't answer.

"Jeff?"

"Hush," came his response. "Stay there."

Since Jeff had never hushed me before, I was oddly obedient. I sat cross-legged on my red sleeping bag, waiting for the car to leave and for Jeff to come into the tent to fill me in on why he told me to hush.

Finally, the vehicle pulled away. There was no movement from Jeff for a while until at last I saw by his shadow, that he doused the fire with water, before unzipping the tent and crawling in, at which time he told me what had incurred.

Apparently, when Jeff went over to see what the problem was, the driver didn't speak to Jeff. He didn't roll down the window, didn't open the back door to let Jeff in, but just pointed to in front of him. About ten feet away, a large brown bear had lumbered onto the road and stopped in the car headlights. As soon as the bear passed, the car left Jeff standing there, all alone in the night, with a huge bear walking along the edge of our campsite and disappearing in the blackness somewhere just out of sight.

Luckily, the big ole lug was not hungry, nor angry, and was just passing through. Needless to say, it took an awfully long time for two adult Carlsons to get to sleep on that particular camping night.

Oh. And that round dumpster across the road from us? We

found out in the morning it was a baited bear trap, a bear trap which this particular bear was too wise or too full to investigate.

Chapter Twenty-seven – Squirrels

For one of his Cub Scout badges, John made a birdfeeder out of a half-gallon milk carton. We hung it in a tree outside our breakfast window where we could watch it, and a few yards from the church building.

Birds never visited, but a particular squirrel did. With his repeat performance, we named Nutty, even though we fed him seeds. Seedy would have been a more appropriate name. To have his daily feast, Nutty crawled up the tree, over the branch, down the string, and sat butt-first in the carton.

***

While in New York, we hosted international students a few weekends so they could visit Niagara Falls and attend an American church. Two of our guests were from Turkey and Greece. The girls were fascinated by the cute squirrels in America. One of the girls was so infatuated that she wanted to take a squirrel home with her. "Wild animal!" I told her. The idea of keeping a squirrel as a pet was beyond my range of thinking.

***

At college in Bowling Green, Ohio, I saw rare black squirrel—a mutant from the grey and fox squirrels. Decades later, when we moved to Battle Creek, Michigan, lo and behold, there were black squirrels running around, imported into the area from South America by one of the Kellogg brothers a century earlier.

Black squirrels are more aggressive than other colored squirrels, and usually stick to themselves except to fight over feeding territory. Although, one year while walking around our Michigan neighborhood, I saw a squirrel that looked like it was clothed. It's bottom half was red while it's upper half was grey. It made him look like he wore pants and a shirt.

***

My first spring in Michigan was frustrating. The previous fall I'd planted over two hundred spring bulbs intending for color to burst forth over our yard. Shortly after planting them, neighborhood squirrels dug up all my crocus and hyacinth and tulips bulbs, the greedy, hungry little critters.

That spring, I had no tulips at all. The squirrels undoubtedly loved those tasty tulip treats. But the crocus and hyacinth flowers bloomed in various parts of the lawn. I dug up many and replanted them in the dirt flower garden where they belonged. But the same thing happened the following fall. The squirrels dug up the bulbs and replanted them. It didn't take me long to accept my new neighbors and realize that spring could be an exciting time, for I never knew where

71

flowers would pop up. It became a spring treasure hunt. I'm pretty sure our squirrels had also forgotten where they had buried them.

***

Several years later, while pulling into our Michigan driveway, I saw a pale gray squirrel laying on its side next to the drive. It hadn't scurried away as we passed so I assumed it was dead. After Jeff parked the car in the garage, I grabbed the shovel and went back to the spot. The squirrel was gone. It was not quite as dead as I had thought. The next day I found the critter in the front yard, upright, but not moving, pale and scrawny, watching me through unblinking eyes. Our bird feeders were in the backyard, where squirrels and chipmunks searched for and fought over the dropped seeds. The front yard was only used to chase each other up and down and around the trees. Sitting there, watching me, I was able to notice this gray-ish squirrel better. With its patchy fur, it looked mangy, weak, sick…and the way it stared at me, scary. We called it Zombie Squirrel.

The following week, it appeared in various places of our front yard, under the azalea bushes by our front door or under an evergreen bush as I walked out to get the mail. It didn't seem to have the strength to climb a tree, so it was always in a low position, and I never saw it move. It just popped up at different locations. Squirrels are naturally hyperactive. Zombie Squirrel's actions were not at all squirrel-ish. Eventually, it found its way back to the bird feeder area, and interestingly enough, instead of chasing it away, the other squirrels kept their distance from Zombie Squirrel. I knew just how they felt.

My first "cattle roundup" happened one November in Wisconsin in the 1970's. I became friends with a Chicago couple trying their hand at getting back to nature by farming. I met them at our small rural church in Caledonia by the Wisconsin River. Their farm consisted of two hundred goats, a large apple orchard, and six beef steer which needed to be moved from their summer pasture to the winter pen by the barn. I'd milked some of their goats, but was so slow that the owner finished milking five goats while I was still working on my first one. The evening before the planned roundup, I ate supper with City-slicker Farmer and his family. Their plan was that after the cattle were moved, they'd drive to Chicago, then flying to Florida the following morning for a two-week cruise.

During our meal together, the hired hand called to inform them there'd been a death in his family. He apologized, but couldn't come for about a week. The orchard was "sleeping" and they'd arranged for someone to milk their goats, but City-slicker Farmer was stuck as far as care for his cattle went.

Being the gullible, adventuresome, and single teacher, I volunteered to tend their cattle, doing chores before and after school until Hired Hand Man returned. How hard could it be? After all, my grandparents had a farm. I didn't tell them my only farming experience consisted of collecting chicken eggs. Once.

It was settled. I'd move into the downstairs spare room after church and before the roundup.

Oh. The family had also taken in a stray pregnant dog staying in their basement, who was "going to give birth any day now." I only had to see her when I fed their wood-burning furnace each morning and evening to heat the house. Feeding the furnace couldn't be too difficult. I'd made campfires before. They kept the outside cellar doors open for the dog so she could come and go at will. From that furnace on their dirt cellar floor, there were only a few odd steps heading up to their unlocked house.

Earlier in the week, City-slicker Farmer had called in some of their city-slicker friends (like me) to help for this simple roundup. All we helpers had to do was be a human barrier to keep the beasts headed towards the barn from their field, a mere hundred yards. He guessed it would take ten or twenty minutes.

Roundup day, we fifteen non-farmers gathered and marched into the field where the cattle suspiciously eyed us newcomers. City-slicker Farmer cautioned us, "They are big and can be dangerous. If one breaks the line and comes towards you, all you have to do is wave your arms above your head to look big and say, 'HA!'"

We lined up in our designated spots in the pasture and along the drive to the barn gate and their winter pen. City-slicker Farmer moved slowly to position himself behind them. He started walking towards us with the cattle walking before him. All was going smoothing and uneventfully when one of the steer came to about twenty feet from one of the city-slicker helpers. The man panicked. He flapped his arms wildly above his head and screamed out, "HA! HA! HA!"

All six steers ran away from City-slicker Farmer and deep into the field. Soon other people left their positions to chase after the cattle. They also waved their arms and shouted, "HA!" People and cattle ran in every direction. I admit, once I actually did say "HA" but only when a wide-eyed steer charged within six feet of me.

By the end of our two-hour-long City-slicker Roundup, only two of the bovines were safely inside their winter pen by the barn. They panted heavily, with eyes about four times larger than they ought to have been. The other four beasts had vanished, undoubtedly still at full run somewhere over the hills of central Wisconsin, becoming very lean meat indeed. The helpers piled into their cars and left.

During the roundup, I'd injured my knee. Seven years earlier, I'd torn a ligament in my right knee, and when I wasn't careful, like hiking downhill for long periods, or running after cattle, I'd feel it. I limped with each painful step to the last car to leave the farm. City-slicker Farmer and his family got into their vehicle.

"We have to go," he told me. "The others will probably show up tonight. Just open the gate and let them in." Then they drove off and left farmer's granddaughter-me alone, along with two steers and one very pregnant dog.

Before bed that Sunday night, I looked outside. In the white glow of the single mercury light lighting the barn area, sure enough, just as City-slicker Farmer predicted, the four lost cattle stood outside their winter pen gate.

I bundled up in my red down jacket and pulled on my hiking boots now covered with manure, and limped out the backdoor. Not wanting to spook the beasts further, I quietly spoke to them starting from the house doorway all the way to the pen gate. Twelve eyes watched me like something from a horror movie. When I opened the gate, to my surprise and delight, the four outsiders trotted in to join their comrades. I broke the ice starting to form on the water in their trough and told them, "Welcome to your winter pen, boys. I hope you have a good night's rest." In fact, every time I left the house or got out of my car when I returned from teaching, I'd talk to those boys in their pen.

Monday, I rose earlier than normal to do my farm hand chores. Breaking the ice in the water trough was harder than the night before because of the thickness built up from the overnight cold. Feeding, however, was a simple procedure. There was a switch on the side of the silo. When I pressed it, feed would jiggle out and shake along the feeding trough. However, City-slicker Farmer had warned me that sometimes he had trouble with it, and if it didn't work, all I had to do was go to the top of the three-story barn, toss down two bales of hay, and spread it along the trough. So, that first morning of chores, I reached over the fence and clicked the nearby switch.

Nothing happened.

I flicked it a few more times just to make sure. Nothing. Not even a hum of machinery trying to work.

I was irritated that I might be late for school from this delay. I hobbled to the top story barn, moaning with every step, and tossed two bales of hay through the opening. Not wanting to frighten them with both the new way to feed and the newcomer feeding them, I talked the entire time to the cattle below, assuring them that by the noises I made, that I wasn't mad at them, but angry with my knee hurting like crazy from the extra climbing.

By the time I got into the pen, the cattle were already eating. I considered just letting them have it, but saw that they all couldn't reach the stringed bales. In I went, sinking to my ankles in the muck. With my shoulder, I shoved as hard as I could against the huge black beast hogging one bale. I moaned in pain as I hoisted the hay and spread it over the tough. Some of the cattle followed me and started in on the hay from the trough. Good steers. I went after the other bale and again shoved the big black beast away, the same one who had hogged the first bale. I snatched it away and spread out that hay, too.

I repeated this morning and evening—feeding the fire, the pregnant dog, the cattle, moaning and talking to animals for three days until that afternoon, Hired Hand showed up, earlier than expected.

He'd felt badly for deserting City-slicker Farmer, and although he knew that City-slicker-teacher-woman was holding down the farm, he wasn't sure what shape things would be in.

As I packed up my belongings, I informed him of the broken silo. He told me it had to be fixed immediately or the feed inside would rot. City-slicker-teacher-woman hadn't thought of that. As fixing it was a two-person operation, I diligently followed him out for my final farmhand chore. He seemed jumpy and told me to watch the cattle. It sounded like a silly request, but I watched them, and they watched me. I spoke to them quietly, being a bit shy talking to animals in front of another two-legged.

Hired Hand climbed into the pen, up the outside ladder, and into the silo, telling me when to click on or off the switch. It looked dangerous. I'd heard farm accident stories, and was certain he was going to fall into the feed from the vibration and smother to death. But he was the expert. I did as I was told. It wasn't long before he got the silo working properly. Hurray! I could leave City-slicker Farmer's cattle in the hands of someone who actually knew what he was doing.

As I limped back to my car, Hired Hand confessed how scared he was of the cattle, which was why he wanted me there while he fixed the silo. One steer in particular charged him every time he went into the in the pen or pasture. He'd often knocked Hired Hand to the ground, standing over him. Hired Hand told me this because he was so surprised with the good and calm behavior of the cattle. This was the first day that one particular bovine hadn't charged him.

I looked at the steer he pointed to. It was the big black one who was always the first to feed on a bale after I'd tossed it from the upper part of the barn. He was the only one I ever had to shove away, morning and evening. I did it because I had a job I'd committed myself to do. My friends and the animals depended on me, and me alone. I was in too much pain at the time to be scared of any big ole steer. Perhaps the cattle knew I was in charge, or in pain, or knew my daily grumbling wasn't because of them, but I took care of them, anyway.

With all my complaining to them, I figured getting injured on my first-ever roundup ended up being a good thing after all.

Thirty – Up to Bat

When I was five months pregnant with our first child we moved from Illinois to a church in Fort Dodge, Iowa, in August. We moved into the church-owned manse (parsonage, rectory) because we didn't have the money for a down payment on a house of our own, and weren't familiar enough with the town to know apartment areas. The church had been trying to sell the manse for over two years with hardly a nibble, not even a low bid. It seemed a reasonable place for us to settle in for a while.

One of our first nights there, while Jeff was off to a night meeting with his new job, I continued my attempt to get the house all ready for the new baby. I'd been working for two hours and realized I was exhausted. I sat down on the couch in the library area, and rested my head back, looking up at the ceiling. A bat flapped to within inches of my face, then darted off into the living room.

I was concerned about being pregnant and rabies-carrying bats. I was so new to town that I didn't have any new phone numbers, and since this was pre-cell phone era, I couldn't call or text my hubby for help (or suggestions). I bolted next-door to my new neighbors to wait for Jeff to come home. Her husband was also gone for the evening. Neither of us felt brave enough to investigate the manse for any maybe-rabies-infected bat. Besides, she had a sleeping five-year-old she didn't want to leave alone. We waited until I saw Jeff's headlights head down the alley and go into the garage. I darted out of her house before Jeff shut the garage door.

I explained what I'd experienced and Jeff and I made a search of the house. I did not want to get rabies! During our search, in order to protect myself, I'd put a sleeping bag over my head and held a badminton racket in my hand, ready to swat at the invader. My husband carried a fishing net loosely at his side. We did a search of the house closing off rooms as we checked them. After we thoroughly checked the master bedroom, we found no other living creature inside the house. Still, Jeff agreed to shut the door to the hallway.

Pre-internet, but being the informed reader, Jeff had read about nervous conditions and hysteria of pregnant ladies. Apparently, he went along on this bat search because his pregnant wife was certainly in hysterics. He wasn't exactly believing me.

It was a warm August night. Our bedroom screened windows were open. We slept with just a sheet over us. About 5:30 AM I heard the undeniable *whoo-whoo-whoo* of wings flapping over our faces. I threw the sheet over both of our heads and screamed Jeff awake with, "WE LOCKED IT IN HERE WITH US!"

Jeff has never been a morning person. It took him a while to figure out why a sheet was over his head and why his hysterically pregnant wife was yelling at him. We carefully peeked over the sheet. There was no bat. Again, poor new husband was worried about his wife's emotional state, but groggily agreed to search the bedroom...again. Only, this time we found it. The night creature clung inside the folds of the curtain between the curtain and the window screen. Jeff tried to shake it loose, but it clung on pretty tightly. We finally decided to take the screen off the window, and slowly pull the curtain over the open window. Jeff took the badminton racket and whacked it out of the house.

Now that we knew there was actually a bat in the house, we figured the only place it could have come in was down the chimney, and how many more would follow? We never found out because after getting rid of all our moving boxes, our previously empty house now had that "lived-in look," and sold within a month.

September 2014, I spoke at a SCBWI (Society for Children's Book Writers and Illustrators) writers conference on Mackinac Island, Michigan. I drove up the day before the conference, checked into a (cheaper) motel on the mainland, and then headed west to find the new Dark Sky Park on the other side of the Mitten's tip where I watched the sunset over Lake Michigan, looked into a powerful telescope, and heard from an astronomer about the stars in the clear sky overhead.

I didn't return to my motel until close to midnight. As I opened my motel room door, a bat swooped in along with me. I kept the door opened for some time, hoping it would both fly out and that none of his relatives would fly in. No result. I woke up the motel owner. Of course, we couldn't find any bat, As I was packing up to move to another room, the tricky bat flew out from behind the curtains, laughing at us, I'm sure. The owner swatted it with a towel, grabbed it, took it outside, and killed it. Killed it! The poor bat. Maybe I shouldn't have awakened a grouchy motel owner.

***

The following night I was on the island at the conference. It was a lovely fall evening, so all the double doors off the main meeting room leading onto the porch were wide open. Guess who joined us? No, not a zombie bat from the night before, but definitely some cousin. The large percentage of SCBWI members are women. So for the next twenty minutes, while our speaker tried to continue her presentation, there were pockets of women who yelped or screamed whenever the bat came within, oh, a hundred yards of them. Finally, the bat left. People immediately shut the doors, because, you know: bats.

And interestingly enough, the only wildlife I could find on Mackinac Island were seagulls, bats, and tourists.

***

In the fourth grade (1990), Peter's instrument of choice was trumpet. We lived in a suburb of Buffalo, New York, with the enchanting name of Cheektowaga (Land of the Flowering Apple Blossoms). That summer we won a week's family scholarship to attend Chautauqua Institution, about ninety minutes from where we lived. This is an amazing educational place.

One of the hot July evenings there, we attended the youth summer band concert in the amphitheater. After the first hour, six-year-old John started wiggling. I decided to walk him back to our boarding house. There wasn't much to do inside the house, and it was hot (no air conditioning), so I thought if we lay on the hill behind the house, on the slopping lawn with huge trees, we could watch stars come out.

It only took seconds before we found something besides stars had come out. Bats! Literally thousands of them dotted the sky above us and swooped within a couple inches of us. In my rational brain I knew bats have this radar thing going on and wouldn't "crash" into

83

us. At first it was difficult to lie still. But we realized we were perfectly safe. The reason for so many bats swarming around us was that our hot bodies attracted mosquitoes which in turn attracted the bats. What an amazing, entertaining and natural mosquito repellant. It was thrilling, lying there as bats and mosquitoes fought their battle of survival over us. We did not get a single mosquito bite. Thank you, and you're welcome, bats.

***

P.S. I am very sad to report that while looking up information about these animals, I found that 90% of the brown bat population in the Chautauqua area has died off since then. Today, there may be a single bat sighting over the lake at dusk. Scientists discovered this reduction of population was caused by mold which covered the animals as they hibernated, disrupting their sleep cycle and thus causing them to wake to winter, and no food.

It reminds me of the early 1990's when I took a solo trip to a SEAL Navy Base in Indiana. I went, not to learn about bats, but to do research for a book on "Old Ironsides," a ship my great-great-grandfather helped design. For on that base there are trees designated for the re-buildings of the oldest commissioned navy ship in the USA, the *U.S.S. Constitution*.

While there, the civilian environmentalist told me many things, including the decline of bats in the various caves on the base. When they conducted a study, they discovered the deaths were caused from the bats who migrated far to the south, eating insects from fields which had been sprayed with pesticides. Sadly, raising food for humans resulted in involuntary manslaughter, or I should say batslaughter.

Chapter Thirty-two – Flying Trail Map

In the early 1990's we Carlsons Four were starting out on a spring hike on a new-to-us trail in the Allegany Mountains of New York. We were gearing up to leave this state and move to South Dakota. The Allegany Mountains were some of our favorite NY stomping grounds.

The trailhead near where we parked had a small rectangular wooden box on a post with the sign above it reading, "Trail Maps." We knew from previous experience that these boxes were usually empty when we chose to hike, which was usually not the busy summer time. People filled the boxes with the maps early in summer. They were gone before Labor Day. But did that bit of personal knowledge stop me from trying to check out the Trail Map Box, anyway? No, it did not. I was hoping to find a map, but expected trash. The three male Carlsons aimed for the trail while I took my little side-trip to check out the box.

I opened the slanted lid on the top and leaned forward to peek inside when something flew out at me. Literally! *Whoosh!* I had to rely on my Carlson men to tell me what it was which sailed past my face in a brown blur. It was a flying squirrel. My heart raced from being startled, but everyone else was buckled over in laughter.

And, no, I did not recheck the box when we finished the hike to see if the squirrel had slipped back in. I thought about it, yes, but check it? No.

Chapter Thirty-three – Chipmunk Horrors

If you are anything like me, you might be of the opinion that chipmunks are cute. For me, that attitude undoubtedly comes from all the Chip and Dale cartoons as a kid. Chipmunks are perfectly striped critters, with amusing antics. They're small enough to hold in your hand if you dared. When gathering seeds, they stuff their little cheeks full with nearly their body weight right in their mouths. It's also fun to watch them quickly darting and zigzagging, chasing each other around in early summer.

That is, I used to think them cute. After a dozen years living in our Michigan house in Battle Creek, in 2016 chipmunks suddenly multiplied in our yard. We used to have squirrels in our backyard. Lots of squirrels. There were your typical Battle Creek black squirrels as well as the grays or browns. We also had bird, raccoon, deer, voles, snakes and opossum. But when the gang of chipmunks settled in, the other animals went elsewhere. Those cute little rascals often kept me from my own backyard.

It's unsettling when normally wild creatures, who really ought to be terrified of giant humans hundreds of times their size, come within a few feet of said giant, weave around you faster than you can follow with your eyes, and even charge at you. They scurried along the chain link fence tops, running parallel to you, and if you stop, they stopped. And stared. They not only eat the bird feed (which we quit putting out, poor birds), but they easily climb trees and into bushes to feast on bird eggs sitting helplessly in their nests. That summer they exploded in population in our yard. At one time I counted twenty of the critters in our small backyard at once. They also ate every one of my tomatoes, even taking bites out of the green ones. Well, there were an awfully lot of little mouths to feed.

I'm guessing that the reason the little fellas were able to be so prolific was because the summer before I'd accidentally killed the largest garter snake I'd ever seen. It had a belly diameter of three inches, and was more than three feet long. It got twisted in the plastic netting I'd put around my young sunflower plants—netting so the chipmunks wouldn't dig up the plants. My guess is that Granddaddy Garter feasted on chipmunks, and when he sadly met his demise, the little rodents were all about eat, drink, and be merry… and have lots of babies.

My problem-solving husband searched the Internet to identify humane ways to rid one of chipmunks. Our jar of fox urine (fox =

natural predator to rodents) arrived after a couple of days. I sprinkled the elixir around their most popular haunts, as well as near the entrance to their holes in the ground. This appeared to do the trick. For two days. Then it rained and washed away our magic potion. It wasn't forecast to rain the next night, so I redid the ritual, singing softly, "What does a Fox Say?" It rained again that night, anyway. Bye-bye fox urine. Hello chipmunks. Again.

Fox urine is expensive.

The following spring, I stuffed sticks into fifteen chipmunk holes in our backyard. New holes appeared. I stuffed in more sticks. I noticed the population of these species had decreased, but some hung around, just a few, about four, I think. Manageable. Although they still eat my tomatoes.

Chapter Thirty-four – Algonquin Provincial Park, 1987-1996

When we lived in Western NY, we could tolerate anything that happened for fifty-one weeks of the year because we knew that on that fifty-second week each year, we'd be in Algonquin Provincial Park, Ontario, Canada, about a six-hour drive north of us. It was well worth the drive, even going through busy Toronto.

The approximately 3,000 square mile park is located along the edge of the Ontario Shield, so has both the northern pines as well as broad-leafed trees. There is only one paved road (56 kilometers) through the park; you can only see the rest of the park via lake (canoeing) or hiking.

Visiting Algonquin over the years, we've seen moose, bear, loon, otter, spruce grouse, beaver, great blue herons, and more.

It's quite different finding or hearing animals in the wild v.s. seeing them in cages of a zoo or even in a sanctuary. For one, there are far fewer animal sightings in the wild; secondly, you come upon them unexpectedly; and thirdly, with no protective walls or cages keeping them from coming at you, the thrill level is higher. It necessitates you to be constantly alert instead of merely being a casually observant.

The week before the boys started school, during the last week of August and over Labor Day Weekend was our Algonquin time. Because we visited at the same time each year, we became friends with our campground's host family, the Dunbars, who also were at the campground the same week as us.

***

One year, just after we got our tent set up and tarp over our picnic table, we noticed a squirrel dropping green pine cones from a fifty-foot tree on our site. He would drop several cones over a few minutes time, allowing them to dive onto our tent and tarp like little bombs. The animal then climbed down the tree, collected them, and took them up to his nest. He continued the pull-and-drop process all over again.

We considered moving our site, but he was ours for the week. Because he was a red squirrel, we named him The Red Barron, a WWII reference of a German bombardier.

***

One year on our first evening at the park, we were in our canoe exploring the far edge of Pog Lake. Canoeing is a quiet activity, at least it was for us. We rarely spoke except to decide where to put in or take out for portages.

We discovered a beaver lodge in the middle of the bay, out of sight from the campground or any trails. We were pointing out to each other the pencil-pointed tree trunks along the shore, left by beavers gnawing, when there came a very loud "slap" close by us which echoed across the lake. We startled so much that we nearly tipped the canoe. We never saw the animal, but knew it was a beaver tail, slapped down on the water, warning us away from his territory.

We got the hint!

***

In Algonquin we often heard loons with their distinctive calls. Using canoes and kayaks, we, too became water creatures sharing the same habitat.

90

We saw loons in flight and with their lengthy dives. You'd never know exactly where they'd surface.

One time, we'd put in at a small creek near the Spruce Bog Trail, the summer the new Visitor Center was being built. We meandered our canoe around the twisting creek to Norway Lake, at which point both Jeff and I assumed each other had the map of the area. We'd planned on going farther, making a day of it v.s. a few hours. We were totally alone on the lake for that entire day. We pulled up at a backpacking site and spotted the thigh-high square box with hinged lid not far from the fire circle, obviously to be used for a very exposing "outhouse." We also knew were we in backpacking country because we saw bear claw scratchings on the nearby trees.

We explored by canoe the entire shore and paused not far from a beaver dam, hoping to spot one. Instead, we found otters—wonderful, playful, delightful otters. They slid down a mud slide next to the lodge, into the lake, and dove under water. Several curious young ones popped up next to our canoe, blowing the water from their whiskers with a "Fwooh." I dug through my waterproof pack for my SLR camera and attached the close-up lens. I pointed it at the water, ready for when one might appear.

Fwoof.

That came from the other side of the canoe. By the time I'd twisted around for the shot, the otter had disappeared back under water. But I was ready for when it would come back up.

Fwoof.

I turned back to the other side of the canoe just in time to see the critter duck under water.

Fwoof. Fwoof.

I'd turn; they'd dive. The three Carlson males shook the canoe with their laughter. I never did get a shot of the sneaky, playful water guys.

***

Another time I wanted a shot of this gigantic frog sitting on a log on the twisting waterway between Pog Lake and Lake of Two Rivers. I got out my camera as Jeff in the stern got me closer and closer. I expected an action jumping shot, but the frog just sat there with its butt facing us. With camera in one hand, I touched the log with my paddle. The frog didn't move. I ever so gently nudged its leg with the paddle. That leg just bent the "elbow" to its side, but otherwise didn't move. We laughed about it being a frog celebrity. "You don't like that back shot of me. How about this one with my dropped shoulder?"

We paddled on.

Chapter Thirty-five – Algonquin Wolf Howls
and a BBC Documentary

Algonquin Park puts on Public Wolf Howls. These have been going on for over fifty years each Thursday night in August. In the amphitheatre, early evening, a park naturalist will give a talk about the Algonquin (smaller-than-other-North-American) wolves with a slide show. Then we'd all pile into our cars and go to the "secret" location, which the naturalists had determined from the previous night, where they'd been able to locate a wolf howl response. On the occasional sad week, when they didn't get a response to their human howls, the Wolf Howl would be cancelled.

By the end of August and when the tourists, like the black flies, were not as many, we'd usually be in one of the smaller groups of the season, about seven hundred cars. Having that many people, standing along Highway 60 in the dark, and keeping silent, was a remarkable feat. The suspense of waiting for the naturalists to finally howl. And then waiting seconds for the response from the pack…spine tingling.

The pack continued to howl for about ten minutes. You could distinguish the difference in the howls, recognizing the yelps of pups over the lower-sounding adult voices. Mere words are impossible to describe the feeling of listening to a pack in the wild. A few: Thrilling. Amazing. Heart-stopping.

Afterwards, when the howling died down and all was silent again, there was a feeling of such joy radiating from the roadsides to have been part of this wonderful wild thing.

***

In 1996, we four Carlsons were some of about 20 people asked to participate in a BBC (British Broadcasting Corporation) reenactment of an Algonquin Wolf Howl. It was a show about wolves around the world, to be shown in 1997 on the Discovery Channel. What a privilege. And a whole lot of fun. The crew from England were very funny and nice folk.

The crew lined up our cars on the edge of the parking lot, woods to the back, representing the side of Highway 60. They wanted us to pretend to be listening to a wolf howl. I can only image our various expressions when they yelled cut, and all us "actors" giggled. We knew they were using filters to represent night, but it was daytime! Plus, we were in a crowded parking lot. Most importantly, there were no wolves to react to!

Finally, some clever Canadian behind the crew started a howl, just like a naturalist would do. We all chuckled again and nodded. That's the way it was done. The BBC director perked up and we did a few repeats of "wolf howl reactions", with the camera flowing down the line of participants. Then they wanted a close up of a family. Enter the Carlsons Four. It may have been because we had a mom, a dad, a teen, and a child. I also wore a denim cap and red flannel shirt, which may have made me look both Canadian camp-ish and stylish for the time. Who really knows why we were chosen? It wasn't difficult to remember the sensation of what it's like hearing wolves in the wild. The director thought what he'd filmed of us was great, and was sure it would be included in the documentary.

After the experience, young John wanted to first be an actor when he grew up, and afterwards a veterinarian. Ah, the effects of showbusiness. Over the following two years, friends across the States and in Canada wrote us (pre-texting days) about seeing us on TV. I was curious to see for myself, but we never were able to catch the program.

A somewhat curious thing for Jeff and me which came out of that experience was that we would never watch another documentary again without wondering what had been staged and what was real. But it was an interesting, once-in-a-lifetime event in a wonderful park, and it had to do with wolves, although no wolf was actually involved in this particular story.

Chapter Thirty-six – Moose Sightings in Algonquin

Often along Highway 60, whenever there was a moose sighting, drivers pulled to the shoulder, causing other drivers to pull over for a look-see as well. The moose proximity to the road was habit from getting salt from when the roads got salted during winter. Yummy salt!

Moose are huge mammals with legs that go all the way down to the ground. Gorgeous. Regal. Majestic animals. People pulled out their binoculars (everyone in the park carried binoculars in their vehicles) and watched the moose. During our ten visits to the park, we usually spotted at least one moose each visit along Highway 60. But without a doubt, it was more thrilling to see them closer up, when we hiked trails through the woods.

Once on a newly-opened-that-summer trail, I nearly bumped into a cow (female moose). The wild animals were still used to that section being their territory and human-free. I was in the lead of our little band of hikers, and didn't even see her until I was about twenty feet away and Jeff whispered to stop.

We Carlsons stood silently watching her eat, fearless of the four humans so near. We recognized the potential power of beast, and the damage which teeth and hooves of a frightened or angry moose could do, thankful it wasn't a bull. Once we spotted it (and were fully aware that she, too, was aware of our presence), we didn't want to move for fear it would spook her. So, we stood silent, watching this massive animal eat for several minutes.

All of a sudden, she jerked her head and straightened up, ears pointed in our direction. None of us had moved. We became more silent than the pines as we, too, became alert and listened. There were bear in Algonquin Park, too. The moose turned from us and trotted away, disappearing into the wilderness. We remained standing where we were, stunned and speechless from witnessing such a majestic creature for so long and so close.

Within a couple of minute, two men and a dog (on a leash) came along the trail from behind us. We were so silent and still that our presence surprised them, but the friendly Canadians smiled and said hi as they passed. I was going to mention something about what they'd just missed, but even if I had managed words, all I might have been able to say would have been, "Moose. Dog."

***

One time on a hike in Algonquin, we saw an oddly behaving moose. It was skittish and seemed scared. For decades, the moose inside the park were safe from hunters, but a couple of weeks earlier, the park opened moose hunting to Natives in the area. This was our best guess as to why it was so skittish.

Chapter Thirty-seven – Bear in Algonquin

The four of us Carlsons and the two Dunbar (host family) teenage girls decided to hike the new Centennial Trail in Algonquin. It is an 11-kilometer trail, so we planned on it taking us four to five hours, with bag lunches along the way.

While in Wyoming, I used to wear bells around my ankles through bear country so as not to startle bear. But with six of us hiking, we made sufficient enough noise, albeit quiet noise, that we couldn't startle a bear.

The Centennial Trail was so new there weren't even nature posts/signs up, nor even a trail brochure. We were about a third of the way around the loop when two young women came running towards the six of us. They were pale and obviously frightened. A mama bear had charged at them and chased them. We invited them to walk with us. We figured the bear would not charge a group of eight humans bunched together, even if she had cubs. The two women were too scared to continue on and backtracked back to the trailhead. But Peter and John looked at each other wide-eyed, said, "Bear!" and started running down the trail.

We all know—even young boys know—it really is rather silly to go running towards a mama bear whom we know recently charged people. Peter and John were our little cubs we wanted to protect. I didn't want to yell at them for fear of getting the bear angry, but I also didn't want to charge down the trail either. It was a bit difficult to get two excited boys to stop.

And then we saw her: Mama bear sat at the base of a tree about thirty yards downhill from the trail. Her two cubs were up the tree she guarded. The six of us watched and whispered how wonderous it was. After a while, one of the cubs climbed down and started nursing.

Nursing! We felt honored for the mama to feel so confident to nurse her baby with human strangers watching.

We were getting ready to leave when an older couple in their 50's came from behind. We motioned for them to be quiet, and pointed out the bear and her cubs. They immediately rummaged through their packs and pulled out two cans of pepper spray.

It felt wrong for many reasons for them to feel the need of pepper spray, but especially after we had been standing there for so long watching this miracle of life unfold before our eyes. We let the couple move on and followed shortly after, allowing Mama bear to regain the peace that she needed.

***

We also learned that summer the way to identify the difference between black bear and grizzlies from their scat (aka, poop). If there are berries and squirrel fur in it, it's most likely black bear scat. On the other hand, it is more likely to be grizzly if the scat smells like pepper and has little jingle bells in it.

***

Another time, hiking a different new trail with our Canadian friends, we came to an area where there was brush about seven feet high on either side of the trail. Over that certain stretch, we kept smelling that yucky skunk smell here and there. Only, our host family teens informed us, in that particular part of Ontario, there are no skunk. They whispered, "Bear give off an odor which smells like

99

skunk." After that, we remained bunched together as we hiked, as all our senses were on high alert. We didn't know if the bear was just out of sight in the brush, or just passed through the area, leaving behind its distinctive smell. Thankfully, there was no close encounter bear sightings for the six of us that day.

Chapter Thirty-eight – Father-Daughter trip to Canada

When I was a little girl my daddy promised me he would take me on a business trip with him as soon as I learned how to curl my own hair. As soon as I learned the trip-taking criteria, I quickly accomplished it. But the timing was never right. Although he'd taken my brother, I never got to go on a business trip with my dad.

When he was in his assisted living facility I brought up that memory. He felt so guilty he suggested, nearly insisting, that he and I go on a trip together. Since I was designated to pick where, and knowing his physical limitations and short-term interest in things, I chose to go to the area where he ran a canoe camp in the early 1950s for high school students. It was near Chapleau, Ontario. We did the circle around the lakes going from Cleveland, Ohio, past Niagara Falls, up north to Chapleau, and then over and down over the Sault Ste. Marie Canal, through Michigan, and back to Cleveland.

There were only two significant wild creatures during that trip, one quite large and the other quite small.

The large one was a moose, of course. Having only experienced moose in Algonquin Park, I never considered what would happen to one trying to get to the other side of the road. Roads up north are very, very long and very, very straight through miles and miles of woodlands, making it easy for people to speed. For the first and only time in my life, I saw in the ditch along the road, four moose legs sticking straight up. I've seen the damage a deer can do to a vehicle, even with the rule: Don't swerve; hit the deer. I cannot imagine how crushed any vehicle (or passengers) would be as a result of speeding into the side of a massive moose. Four legs up.

***

The road we traveled to get near where Dad ran his camp did not exist in the 1950s. People either had to paddle into the camp by canoe or fly in by seaplane. The camp consisted of three buildings, now reverted to wilderness. One dirt road relatively close to the old camp area supposedly had a bridge getting nearer. We traveled over what one could only assume was a logging road and finally met the first two humans outside of any city or town. They appeared to be doing some logging with a chainsaw. I think they were a man and woman, possibly mother and son. It was difficult to tell with the mosquito netting hats covering their faces. I rolled down the window to talk. They did not even politely lift up the netting, but spoke through it. Mosquitoes surrounded our car, and them, and came into the car as

101

I asked them about the camp area. "Can't go that way." The bridge was washed away decades before. We turned around and went back to the main road. I wondered what their conversation was like after we left concerning those odd, lost Americans.

We passed a sign by a little bridge over a ravine with a river at the bottom. Although we couldn't see anything but the ravine, the sign read "Green Lake." Dad's memory of Green Lake was, "It was so clear you could see a dime lying thirty feet down on the bottom of the lake."

I imagined, here in the still-wilderness, the lake would still be pristine. Dad craved to see the lake once again, and I was curious. Even when I pulled to the side of the road, we couldn't see the lake through the trees. The two of us walk down a very steep bank to get to the wooded lake shore. It was stunningly gorgeous, just as Dad had recalled from fifty years earlier. There were still no buildings along the lake, and probably none within dozens of miles (or kilometers). I could have spent the rest of the day there on the shore of beautiful Green Lake if it were not for one tiny little thing. Or several tiny little things. Within seconds, mosquitoes found us. I figured we were the only creatures with blood for miles and miles (rather, kilometers and kilometers).

Dad and I brushed them away, but soon there were hundreds around each of us, covering us in their mosquito fur and vying for our blood. We started scrambling back up the steep hill. I frantically waved my arms around my 7head and told Dad I would go ahead so that I could unlock the car door. We used keys back then instead of the fobs of today with which you can unlock cars from a distance. He yelled at me to come back and help him. But he was strong. He was a man. It was hard enough for me to swim through the horde of insects without pausing to help him. Turns out, I only beat him to the car by about ten paces, barely getting his door unlocked before he shoved me aside to climb in.

We sat in the car for about fifteen minutes killing mosquitoes who'd made in inside with us. I do believe we lost about three pounds of blood each during that five-minute scurry back to the car.

Chapter Thirty-nine – New Cats, Old Cat, and a Dog

In 1969, when I was an adult of 18-years-old, I joined V.I.S.T.A. (Volunteers in Service to America, now renamed AmeriCorps). On my own and in a new state, I decided I needed a pet. There were two male brother kittens for free, so I took them both into my basement apartment, one of three basement apartments in the giant multi-apartment-ed house in Des Moines, Iowa.

The kittens were only indoor cats, and my apartment, small: one living room/bedroom, and a kitchen in the hallway leading to the bathroom. My bed pulled down out from doors in the living room wall. Each night, as soon as I got down the bed, those hyper kittens started running wild. They knew what was coming. I'd take off my shoes and socks at the last possible moment before jumping into bed because those two little guys liked to lick my bare toes, and I was horribly ticklish. It didn't take the kittens long to figure out they, too, could dash under the covers. I quickly learned to pull my legs crisscross under me and watched the two little lumps zig-zag around the bed, searching after my very ticklish feet.

***

My job changed, so I moved in with another VISTA Worker my age, in "The Bottoms," close to the Des Moines River. Also in the house lived a big, fat, lazy beagle, inherited from a previous VISTA Worker, as well as an old neighborhood tom cat which my housemate had taken in.

Moving day was a neighborhood event. The local kids gathered to see the new VISTA person along with each thing she carried in. They freely walked into, around, and out of the house, a legacy from previous VISTA folk, rather like a community house. The living room was big enough for a couch, one chair, and a small desk and chair. The bedroom, big enough to hold bunk beds and no dresser, was actually a hallway leading to the bathroom and kitchen.

That day, my two cats were terrified with the people and noise and newness. It didn't help that the Big Old Fat Beagle, who hardly moved even to eat, barked at them. They remained on the top bunk for the entire moving portion, hissing at everyone who passed. Finally, I got all my stuff in and the neighborhood kids were shooed out, but still lingered in the dirt yard.

After a while, the bolder of my two cats decided to venture off the top bunk. It headed towards the front door, but since my cats had never been outside in their lives, I wasn't letting them out. But the cat meowed so pitifully that I finally relented and opened the screen door. My young cat stretched out his neck and sniffed. Then the BOF beagle sneaked up behind him and barked once. I failed to shut the screen in time as my cat shot through the opening, with BOF beagle barging through after it.

My cat leapt onto the nearest tree and scurried up. He sat trembling on a high branch. I didn't even realize he knew how to climb. Instinct, I guessed. Terror. Flight to safety. There he was, stuck in a tree about three times as high as the peak of our rooftop. I pulled the dog back into the house so it wouldn't be a distraction. Even though it was dark, and there were no streetlights in this area of town, the neighborhood kids still lingered with the new environment. My neck got sore looking up at my poor baby stuck so high. I tried to sound calm as I urged him to come. The neighborhood kids also called to him, as well as jumped about, as well as asked me if I was going to call the fire department to get him down. Welcome to the neighborhood!

Through all this, from behind me, the old tom cat cried at the front screen door. I ignored him for as long as I could, but he made such a continuous fuss that I relented, again, and let him out. It couldn't get worse. So, what did that old tom do but shoot right up that tree where my little cat was. I was certain Old Tom would swat him off the branch, or eat him, or worse.

Old Tom quickly reached the branch where my kitten was stuck, and then, to my surprise, Old Tom started backing down the tree. My cat remained where he was. Old Tom went back up to my kit and backed down again. At last, the younger cat followed suit and backed right down the tree alongside of Old Tom. Reaching the ground, they both raced for the house door as I held the screen to let them in. That day my respect for that old tom cat shot higher than any neighborhood tree could grow.

***

About six months later, I invited a young man into our house. I'd only just met him. I left him to use our bathroom. While in there, I heard a cat screaming and our BOF Beagle barking; odd, because BOF Beagle hadn't uttered a sound since the day we moved in.

I went out to find the man cornered with the beagle not letting him budge.

"What happened?"

"I thought it would be funny to swing one of the cats around by its tail," he replied.

I didn't even ask which one. I reluctantly held back the wonderful, growling BOF beagle while the pervert made his escape, never to be seen again. (Thank goodness.) I hugged BOF Beagle something fierce. He was my BOF hero, and who undoubtedly had protected me, too, from something very bad that could have happened from someone who was cruel to animals.

While living in Michigan, it had rained hard and steadily for several hours. Jeff and I stood on our front porch in the night to watch the downpour. Suddenly, we spotted two creatures, kind of looking like waist-high, skinny greyhound dogs walking on tippy toes, and coming up from across the street from the lake area. It was difficult to tell what animal they were. They were obviously drenched and looked furless. Not being able to identify them made them seem more alien than anything earthly.

As these two critters approached the higher ground where our house lay, we two two-legged animals decided it might be time to make a hasty retreat into the safety of our building. Because…we weren't 100% certain what they were. And who knew what the soaked aliens' intention may be if they spotted us observing them and thought we might expose their existence?

Somehow, we determined that the only creatures they could be were raccoons. We knew some occasionally lived in the drainage pipe going from our yard, under the road, and down toward the lake.

Chapter Forty-one – Bandits, Part I
From California to New York

Raccoons are cute-as-a-button nocturnal animals you just want to hug—if not for the fact, they are wild or that many carry rabbis. Their bandit masks label them accurately. Camping and hiking in woods and living in wooded areas have given us a lot of raccoon contact.

<u>From California</u> – on our honeymoon (1978)

Not far from San Francisco, we backpacked in to a mountainside campground, only about a mile from where we parked our car. It was a place to sleep and eat for the night. There were dozens of sites in this campground. Most were split-level, where you'd pitch your tent on one flat spot with just enough room for a small tent, and below it on a lower flat spot there was just enough room for a picnic table.

As Jeff and I started our supper, in the next campsite below us, about twenty feet away, a group of four rowdy young men set up their tent. They put their cooler inside the tent along with their camping gear and grocery bags. We figured we were in for a long, noisy, party night. But they zipped up their tent and left.

Once again, it was silent there the mountain.

While we two still ate in the light of approaching dusk, a

family of raccoons toddled up to our neighbors' tent. It only took a few seconds for those furry bandits to wrangle their way inside. We debated whether to chase them, but realized that would entail an all evening victual. So, for our dinner theatre mountain entertainment we watched as the raccoons each took something away—a loaf of bread, a box of cereal, rolls, and even items from their cooler.

I was a little nervous with it getting darker by the minute with several raccoons lurking so nearby. Like backpacking-normal, we hoisted up our packs (with any food) high into the trees and started a campfire. The thing with campfires is that you can only see what is in the lighted circle. We went to bed earlier than normal, mostly because I was so nervous. It's funny how I felt perfectly safe in our tent as though it were made of cinder blocks. Besides, we never even took gum or even breath mints into our tent at night for fear the sweetness would attract wild animals.

In the middle of the night, we heard the young men return. We assumed they'd been out drinking. The first thing they would have noticed would have been a trail of paper and plastic garbage around their site. The second would have been the four inch opening to their tent zipper. Flashlights were shooting all over the place. We lay silently in our cinder block tent, waiting to hear their reaction. I thought they'd be drunk-mad, but thankfully not. They soon guessed who the bandits must have been, and were laughing about it. (Lesson learned.)

New York state is populated. There are also many wild animals who have learned to live with the two-legged ones both in the woodlands and in residential areas.

One day our family drove to Letchworth State Park, where there is "the Grand Canyon of the East." The four of us sat eating our lunch at one of the tables in the picnic area. Along came three women with four children. The women were rowdier than the kids. With the fifteen other tables to choose from, they chose the one closest to us, next to the woods.

Soon, from out of those woods, a raccoon immerged. I'd never seen one of the nocturnal critters walking around at high noon. (Can you spell nervous?) We kept our eyes on it as it inched closer. We ate quicker. A few minutes later one of the women at the table near us spotted it, too. Their kids wanted to pet it! They obviously had little wilderness experience. As the kids approached it, the raccoon backed away. The women called the children to return to the table…in order to give the them sandwich bread to feed it! The kids tossed some of the bread at the raccoon who greedily ate it up. It inched nearer. They tossed more food at it, which it quickly consumed.

By this time, although we were only half-way through our lunch, we Carlsons gathered up our food and belongings and headed for our car. We didn't want to wait to see if the raccoon was rabid or not, but probably not or it would have acted even more oddly. As we walked, the women and children screamed. I looked back to see the people standing back in a circle around their table. The adults were waving the backs of their hands at the animal and saying "shoo" as the raccoon sat in the middle of their picnic table eating from their plates from the feast to which the High-noon Bandit had been invited. (Lesson learned?)

Chapter Forty-two – Bandits, Part II
Iowa, Arkansas, and New York (again)

<u>Iowa</u> – in spring, 1971

My friend Marty worked a job with weekends off. So did I. We'd take drive away from Des Moines for a weekend of hiking and camping in nearby state parks. We didn't intend to, but we'd often confuse the park employees registering us because we had neither tent nor RV. There wasn't a spot on the registration sheet for people just plopping sleeping bags on a hill.

One night, I heard Marty shout out my name angrily. Then I *oof-ed* as I felt a pressure on my stomach. I thought she'd punched me. Perhaps it was a nightmare. But when she continued to blame me for something, I informed her that something had walked over me, too. She didn't believe me, not until we heard noise at our picnic table. She shone her flashlight to find an enormous raccoon trying to open the cooler we had left on the table.

We yelled at the critter.

No response.

We tossed some nearby stones at it, but they never reached it. He didn't decease from his task of getting into the cooler.

We climbed out of our sleeping bags, waved our arms and shouting. As we approached it moved to the picnic table bench. We pounded on the table until it lumbered off. We snagged the cooler, rushed it to the car, debated whether or not to sleep the rest of the night in the car, but one of us would have to sleep around a cooler. We returned to our sleeping bags and stared at the stars until the sky lightened up with the dawn. (Lesson learned.)

<u>Arkansas</u> – on our honeymoon

While in Lake of the Ozarks State Park, we cooked up a particularly awful-tasting packet of dried food. Thankfully, we'd only bought one of those packets. After a couple bites, Jeff said to throw it out. At the time (Reduce, Reuse, Recycle), I was reluctant to toss anything away, so decided to leave it on the picnic table for the raccoons to eat. (In my defense, this was early on in my wildlife encounters.)

When we woke the next morning, we noticed lots of muddy little raccoon prints all over the table, but every bit of that awful-tasting meal had also been rejected by our visitors in the night, and remained untouched by the furry food critics.

<u>New York</u> – in our residential Amherst neighborhood

One summer as a new mom living two doors down from us changed her baby's diaper near the open window. A raccoon climbed and clung to the screen just inches from them. She screamed, grabbed her infant and took her to the hallway, shutting the baby's door, then called the city. That same day (hurray for Amherst quick responders) men came to our street to set traps with chicken in them, lowering the traps into our street's sewage drains.

For each of four days, the chicken meat disappeared. The tricky raccoon was not fooled. The men tried a different trap, and at last took away the culprit. Or a culprit. At least we had no more neighborhood raccoon trouble.

Chapter Forty-three – Bandits, Part III – Michigan

<u>Michigan</u> – Battle Creek, early 2000's.

Jeff and I bought a ranch house in a quiet oak forested neighborhood. Across the street from us to the south was a wooded lot and a lake. On the west and north side of us was also a wooded lot. Next door to the east lived a family of four, two adults and two teens. The next-door mom told me they never cooked at home. They used take-out for breakfast, lunch, and supper. Consequently, each week their four larger-than-our-one garbage cans would overflow. They kept their trash cans along the outside side of their garage, about thirty feet from our bedrooms. Because they used them so often, they never secured the lids. We kept our trash can in our garage.

Because of this daily habit, fast food wrappers and styrofoam containers scattered between our houses, trash which they left lie all week until their lawn care people pick it up, at least the trash on the neighbor's property. It was rather disgusting. I can't blame the raccoons who feasted on their garbage each night. But since the humans providing them food were our next-door neighbors, I didn't want to make enemies of them.

Our neighbors finally recognized there was a problem, so used a motion sensor light above the trash cans. When my elderly mother stayed at our house for a couple of nights, the first night she complained, "Your neighbors sure do party a lot. There were headlights shining in our window (with blinds down) all night long as people came and went." After the second night, she woke and mentioned how she dreamed about being in a lighthouse.

I put black plastic trash can liners in our bedroom windows to block the flashing light, but that didn't stop the noise from the partying raccoons each and every night, eight months out of the year. It felt like their motion-sensor light just caused the raccoons to say, "Why, thank you for letting us see what we're eating."

Even with the light, our neighbors recognized there was still a problem, so they hired someone to trap the critter. After the first night, they trapped a raccoon. Second night, they trapped another. Third night, they trapped a third. The forth night, guess what? Yep, they caught a forth one. The sad thing was that one of these trapping days I saw a family of three baby raccoons clinging to a tree just over our property line. I wondered if their parents were now gone, and if the young ones would survive.

Our neighbor complained to me that it cost a lot of money for each animal to be trapped and removed, and that they were doing the job of the neighborhood, indicating that maybe the neighbors (like us) ought to help pay for the trapping and removing of the woodland critters living in our woodland neighborhood. I wanted to say, "Just secure your trash can lids" but I'd already complained about their mean lawn care people who were elderly friends of theirs, and of their permanent outside light which pointed not into their backyard, but into our living room picture window.

Eventually the raccoon problem was solved when the neighbors moved, because, guess what? The new neighbors do not leave their trashcans outside their house, and when they move the cans to the curb, they are covered and locked. The new neighbors have also never used the motion-senor light, and they only turn on the backyard light when they take their dog out at night. After moving in, they immediately turned the backyard light to point into their own yard, without even a comment from me. (Good two-legged neighbors.)

On our honeymoon in 1978, for the 4th of July weekend, we wanted to pick a campground far away from the crowds. We traveled from the main highway to a two-laner, and finally onto the fifteen miles of gravel-dirt road climbing into the eastern Uinta Mountains of Utah. The dirt road to the campground was twisty and pitted enough that you couldn't go faster than 25mph. When we arrived there, we were surprised to find all the wooded campgrounds full. Also, the six football field's length of meadow near the dam was packed with about four hundred RVs. Guess this was where everyone from Salt Lake City came to get away from the crowds. But for us: Crowded!

We were dumbfounded on where to set up our tent for three days in a very busy and noisy campground. Near the woods, on the far side of the meadow, we spotted a Youth Conservation Corps Camp. We went there for suggestions on what we should do. They told us the meadow was normally empty. We asked if we could leave our car near their area while we went off backpacking, returning in three days. They willingly agreed, telling us they'd keep an eye on it. I made a rough pencil map of their map of the area and we shouldered our backpacks. We eventually hiked above the tree line and guessed where the trail was. There was still snow up in this altitude, even on the Fourth of July, so the trail was iffy.

The second afternoon, we found this lovely flat island

meadow. It was lush and green. After we set up our pup tent, we assumed we must have trespassed in the territory of a male elk who eyed us threateningly for hours from a not too distant spot, until it became too dark to see him any longer.

We became lost, because the drawing I'd done made it seem as though we followed the trail, but turned out to be either deer or elk paths. Heading down mountain, I crossed parallel right over the trail. Luckily, smart Jeff looked not only ahead, but to the sides and saw a tree marked with a blue painted dot indicating the trail.

After a wonderful and peaceful three days and nights without sighting or hearing any other human, we returned to the campground, rested and happy, only to find it deserted, except for our lone car left at the now empty Youth Conservation Corps Camp and one RV parked way down near the dam.

Realizing the Rapture had not come, but quite curious, we put our backpacks in the car and casually walked down to ask what happened. The man pointed across the lake to the billowing brown and yellow clouds below us, blocking the direction of the only road out.

"Wildfire," he said.

I thought it safer for us to stay. Jeff wanted to leave. We ran back to the car.

We kept our eyes on the billowing dark sky, driving sometimes away from it, sometimes parallel to it, and us in a car which had broken down several times on our trip, praying this wouldn't be one of the times bumping over the dirt road when it would fail us.

We noticed animals running alongside us. I've seen the look of startled or scared deer, but these held the expression of sheer terror. The deer obviously felt safer running in a herd, even if part of the herd were people inside a car. We were all in this together, dashing for safety.

Then, the road turned. We had no choice but to follow it. The deer ran beside us for a few galloping steps before they veered off. After watching them leave, I looked ahead. The road led straight into the fire. Jeff didn't slow down. I continued praying, knowing that by this time, the road behind us also may be cut off. When we were near enough to see the trees in flame a few yards away, and even feel the heat, the road turned once again, this time parallel to and then, thankfully, away from the fire.

I prayed our deer herd also made it to safety.

We never learned how that fire started. One thing we do know is that the massive wildfire was not started by lightning. But it been a clear weekend, and dry, with many, many Fourth of July revelers. On our three-day backpacking time, although we never saw anyone, we did come across a campfire on the mountain inside a circle of rocks. No one else was around, but it was still smoldering. We stopped our hike long enough to douse it completely with water, and stay until we were certain there were no warm embers. People!

At four years old, I learned to ride horses at Shaker Day Camp. I only rode three times per week, and only the few weeks I was at camp. It was never often enough. When I turned twelve-years-old, I worked at the camp as a junior counselor for five dollars a week (i.e., $1/day), and thus ended my summer riding times, that is, until in high school and old enough to drive to a riding stable.

*****

About five of us from high school decided to rent horses one Saturday. I was the last to be saddled up. By the time the owner had my horse saddled, my friends had vanished. There was a large meadow and beyond that woods where there were several trail entrances. I couldn't tell which one they'd taken, so my horse and me spent time racing in the meadow. I'd never galloped before. I'd only ridden in corrals or walked trails. There was so much freedom to speed. It was glorious.

At a turnaround point (i.e., fence), I noticed a significant hole in the ground, undoubtedly made by some animal. That put an end to my wild meadow speeding. I didn't want to be responsible for my horse to break her leg by into a hole that deep.

After a while, my friends reappeared in the meadow, asking what happened to me. The hour was up and it was time to return the animals to their stalls.

I also need to add in this horsey section a bit about my junior high and high school "Cuz" (so named because we looked alike). Dale went to a different day camp than I did, and later had a job in the stables, including year-round.

In high school, a friend asked me to talk to Dale because "her locker smells like horse." It was true. I sucked my teeth and reluctantly agreed to speak to her.

"Your locker smells like horse," I told her.

Her face lit up in a huge grin. She answered, "I know! Isn't it great?"

About thirty years after our high school graduation, I was able to visit with Dale and her 4- and 2-legged family. She ran an equestrian school for girls. I was overwhelmed with her knowledge and care and love of her small herd and her ability to pair the personalities of the riders to the personalities of the assigned horses. I'd seen the movie "Horse Whisperer" while in South Dakota, where there are plenty of horses. But that story and acting was like a comic book compared to my own true Horse Whisperer, Dale. She has graciously helped me with some of my fictional writing involving horses (and unicorns). She replies with her perfect horse sense.

I was in Brownies and then Girl Scouts until tenth grade, when, during my first meeting, the girls of my new troop voted to wear their Scout uniforms every day during National Scout Week. Sadly, I was too fashion-conscious, and not devoted to this new troop with older girls, that it was my one and only meeting with them. But my scouting experience (especially the outdoors stuff) made me later volunteer to be a Girl Scout Troop leader for three different troops in two states. What fun to pass on the love of the out-of-doors.

In Wisconsin, I piled four girls from my troop in my car while a parent drove the other six girls. We were going horseback riding.

The sky was grumbly and black. The horses, skittish—probably because of the coming rain and sensing the inexperienced youngsters scared to ride them. I questioned the owner if it was a good idea to take them out with the coming storm. He assured me it would be fine. Only one of the girls had been on a horse before. She willingly took the lead. The parent-driver remained behind while I followed the girls and horses into the woods, taking the rear in order to make sure no one got separated. I well-remembered that feeling of being left behind. So off we rode into the storm, just me and ten nervous ten-year-olds.

We'd climbed up the hill and within moments were out of sight of the stables and into the deep, dark Wisconsin woods when the sky opened up. It began pouring. We were somewhat protected in the woods, but it was really coming down. I reached into my daypack to take out my plastic rain poncho. A stupid idea, I quickly realized. My horse, already skittish and uncertain with the storm and scared girls, shied at the rattling sound on her back. That hop caused me to drop the poncho. My horse jumped, poor girl. I hadn't intended to further spook her.

We rode on for a while. We were getting wetter by the minute, but fine. That is, until a loud thunder clasp sounded nearby, and rumbled through the hills. One of the girls screamed. Interesting ten-year-old girls' fact: when one girl screams, the others tend to follow suit. The already fidgeting horses spooked not just with the weather, but now with screaming girls on their backs. We took off at a fast trot.

I yelled—calmly, so as not to add to the frightened mood—to try to get the lead girl to stop. She couldn't hear me over the screaming. I tried to get around the other horses, but couldn't pass on the narrow trail. I shouted-sang slowly and firmly, in the calmest voice I could muster, "Stop screaming, girls. You're scaring the horses."

"We're scared, too," a brave soul responded.

By this time, several girls were crying.

"Pull back on your reins to stop," I sang out. "Pat your horses and talk to them."

It took a while, but finally we were all stopped with the girls obediently patting their horses. Instead of talking, they whimpered at the animals between sobs. And it continued to rain.

Despite how sure the stable owner was that this was safe, I made the decision to cut our ride short. I turned my horse around and instructed the girls how to do the same…and to keep talking to their steeds. I was in the lead this time, making certain we would stay at a walk even if another thunder clasp came. I sat mostly sideways in the saddle as I tried to make happy faces to the girls as well as make sure we all stayed together.

Things were going smoothly with both horses and girls, until we neared the spot where I'd dropped my poncho. When my poor horse spotted that scary, rattly thing, she jumped right off the path to avoid it, crushing my leg against a tree.

By the time we returned to the stable, out of the shelter of the woods, the rain poured on us in the open. The parent-driver waited inside her car.

We checked that off our Scouting badge requirement and didn't go riding as a troop again.

Chapter Forty-six – Dakota Steeds

Our family lived in Rapid City, South Dakota for about ten years. Our boys graduated there from both high school and college.

South Dakota is divided in a number of ways, the most obvious is the Missouri River dividing the green and crop-farming East River from the treeless prairieland ranchers West River, i.e., modern cowboys. Also, about one-fifth of the state is Indian Reservation. Some Indian friends I knew on the Pine Ridge Rez were cattle ranchers, so they were honestly cowboy-Indians. (More on that in the roundup chapter.)

Concerning South Dakota horses, there wasn't a single horse

Jeff or I saw during that decade in all of Western South Dakota (a.k.a., West River) who wasn't stunningly beautiful. Nor did we see a single abused or neglected horse. Having the backdrop of the Black Hills helped esthetically, but really, the animals themselves seemed flawless.

Jeff and I first went horseback riding outside the tiny town of Nemo. It's in a lovely red-rocked valley surrounded by pine woods and blue-blue skies. Our guide took us bushwhacking (off-trail riding). I was thankful I'd purchased a leather cowboy hat a couple of years before that, which I wore upon my head. When going through the scrubs, I lowered my head and let my sturdy Minnetonka hat protect me from the branches. Slick.

Another year, we took our son John and Jeff's college friend Ross riding at the same stables. Ross had been on a horse a few times before, but only trail riding. He wore a cowboy hat he'd bought in South Dakota, but his horse kept jerking her head up and walking backwards. Ross's white-fisted grip on the reins over the horse's neck was about three-quarters shorter (and tighter) than it should have been.

"Loosen your grip," I bossed at him.

He didn't answer the first couple of times.

"It will run away," he finally answered.

We'd saddled up out in the open. No railings. No fences. Just the Black Hills all around us. We'd just be walking, anyway, following our guide. No trotting. No galloping. And not a thunder cloud in sight.

"Even if you dropped the reins," I tried to explain, "your horse will simply follow the horse in front of her."

I know he didn't believe me because he still held a tight hold on the reins.

"Look at mine," I encouraged, dropping my reins. My horse didn't move.

Ross glanced away from his wild steed to peek. He loosened his grip a little. The horse still looked uncomfortable with the tight reins, but no longer backed up. Off we went uneventfully into the Black Hills.

***

Purple bergamot mint was in bloom during one of the times we rode. Our Nemo guide informed us that the horses loved the mint, so people there in the West referred to it as Horse Mint.

One time while out hiking, I easily recognized the square-stemmed plant. Hiking in Canada or other parts out east, we would often chew on a wild mint leaf to refresh our breath. It tasted good, too. So, I put a horsemint leaf into my mouth and started to chew on it like I'd done many times before elsewhere. Only, this time, my tongue swelled up. I never again chewed on one of the leaves. (Tough horse tongues!)

***

While visiting the Badlands of North Dakota in Teddy Roosevelt National Park, Jeff and I went horseback riding again. The terrain there is quite different from the Black Hills or the South Dakota

125

Badlands. Plus, there were wild horses throughout the park. Back in South Dakota had wild donkeys left behind from gold rush days. Wild horses seemed more…wild. There in the ND Badlands, our riding guide told us to veer away from the wild ones. Horses are herd animals, and sometimes, the domesticated, tamed ones got an irresistible urge to join their herd.

Chapter Forty-seven – Shaker Day Camp
Horses and Dragons

The five- and six-year-old camp at Shaker Day Camp was separated from the older kids. To get there, the buses came onto the gravel drive and stopped just past the horse pastures where the campers were dropped off. You walked down the drive with woods on the left and the new lodge (built in the early 1960's) to the right, where the cafeteria was and the owner's son and family lived. If you kept going straight down the hill, there'd be spots over the large open grass area where campers would gather by age groups, and you'd eventually run into the lake. The driveway turned to the left and "ended" at the owner's large house and garage. The "road" continued over a large wooden bridge over a creek and narrowed into a path through the woods. The nurse's station and crafts place were in the basement of the owner's house. If it was a rainy day, campers watched movies in the garage. With your back to the garage, you'd follow a fence along the creek and cross a little bridge, and there you were, at the five- and six-year-old campsite.

There was a little shed where the leaders stashed their daypacks and were able to change into swim suits. This section of camp had its own swimming area near the end of the creek, with a small swampy area with cattails in it on the other side. There was a boy's changing tent and a girl's changing tent, each with four canvas walls around a raised wooden platform with benches along the walls. No roof. Two of the older horses were brought down from the barn led by older campers for riding time. The children climbed onto the horses from a massive tree stump. The riding instructor then told the kids on horseback (two at a time) what to do.

When I was one of those older campers, I'd like to break away from my age group for the opportunity to lead the horses for the little kids. One time I was leading my favorite horse in camp, Alaska. Walking around the grassy loop between the younger kids' camp and the owner's house, we stopped. It wasn't an exciting ride, and we never trotted. I turned to "my" horse. He had his mouth opened in a yawn. Yep. Just walking in circles was boring. But yawns on animals are always so cute. So, I opened my mouth and said, "Aww—" just as Alaska sneezed into my face, and mouth.

***

While working (I should say playing) in the five- and six-year-old camp as a junior counselor, I spotted the cattails in the swampy area. My mother loved cattails. I figured I'd take her home a present that day. I stood at the edge of the ten square foot area with one of the campers. There were large dragonflies flitting about. I took a step in. My heavy weight (all of less than one hundred pounds at the time) caused my shoes to sink. The cattails were just out of my reach. My brave little camper friend offered to go in to get me one. She took two steps and didn't sink into the marsh in the least.

She reached for a cattail and said, "Ow." My mind raced as to why. There were only soft things in a marsh, except for snakes and turtles and crawfish. Then the girl started screaming "ow" over and over. I reached in and grabbed her out. Dragonflies hovered over her, stinging her.

As I swept the child into my arms, they continued to swarm her—but not me. I brushed them away and ran carrying her, over the little bridge, up past the horse riding loop, to the owner's house basement and the nurse.

The girl had swollen red marks over her face and arms. I didn't have a single bite. The nurse took care of the girl who was fascinated with all the attention, and was soon laughing. I still shook.

I never knew dragonflies to be dangerous. Their name took on a whole new meaning. I since learned they have nicknames of "Devil's Darning Needle" and "Horse Stingers." This was the only person I've ever known to be bitten by a dragonfly. One article said dragonflies get agitated when they're laying eggs. However, my fantasy mind (dragons and all) made me wonder if there wasn't something special about this child, something unique flowing through her veins which attracted them.

Chapter Forty-eight – Backpaddling off the Erie Canal

When we lived in Buffalo, New York, and our boys were old enough to be in school, and I had a day off, and Jeff had a day off, we would get out and play!

One school day we canoed, just the two of us, along the Erie Canal. The Canal is long and straight Occasionally it has locks, and usually has roads running next to it, making those traffic sounds.

We decided to take a side creek to get away from civilization noise, and paddled up that way for a while through some farmland.

I was in the bow, with Jeff in the stern, as usual. The creek became shallower and shallower, about shin deep, as well as narrower and narrower. We knew we wouldn't be able to turn around, but continued on. We ducked under overhanging branches and pushed our way over others. On either side of this creek were slight hills, only as tall as our eye level. Beyond the brushy creek area lay farmland. Earlier we'd seen a large pasture with barns it got too narrow. It was quite an adventure...until...I suddenly smelled something "funny." We were already paddling so slowly and cautiously around and over the branches. Being a whole fifteen feet behind me, Jeff didn't smell anything unusual.

As the smell became enhanced, I told him to slow down even more. Then I threw my hand over my mouth and nose, hardly able to breathe. I located the source, half in the water and half out: the decaying carcass of a very large hog about half the size of our canoe. By the time I spotted it, the tip of our canoe bow was coasting to nearly touching it.

"Backpaddle!" I screamed, gagging on the breath required to yell out that one word.

Jeff was confused, but only for a moment until the stern of the canoe came into the aromatic cloud of decomposition.

We moved surprisingly quickly, considering there was no space to turn around and all the branches which we so cautiously crossed early, we now flew over, backpaddling madly. We were soon out of the range of the smell—a smell awful enough that if were we to have remained near it any longer, my eyeballs would have melted.

As soon as the creek allowed, we u-turned that canoe, and stuck to the familiar urban waterway of the Erie Canal.

Chapter Forty-nine – Williamsville Fowls

One of John's sixth grade classrooms in Williamsville, NY, overlooked an enclosed courtyard. That spring, a mother duck hatched fourteen babies, seemingly safe and secure within the walled area. The students enjoyed watching them. But one day someone else started watching them. A hawk. Over the next fourteen days, that hawk flew into the courtyard and took one chick a day to the screams and protests of sixth grade girls.

***

One rainy spring in Williamsville, NY (suburb of Buffalo), I looked out my kitchen window and watched a mallard duck fly toward our lawn. It was aiming for a large puddle in the middle of our backyard. The puddle undoubtedly looked like a small pond to the duck. However, the water was only about one-inch deep. When the duck reached it, his chest splashed onto the ground, and he did a forward somersault. It was not a good place for a water landing.

***

A few blocks away from our house was a stream which included a waterfall over a dam. The stream went under the main road through town. On one side of the road, above the waterfall was a widened area of water with a park. On the other side of the street at the lower part of the waterfalls, the stream meandered around islands and rocks within another park. Often to get from one body of water to

131

the other, instead of flying off the dam, ducks would cross the road from one park to the other. Unfortunately, especially each spring, they were numerous roadkill ducks along that particular stretch of road. Very sad.

I used this visual for a title of a fictional book we had a murder mystery game: *The Williamsville Duck Splat Mysteries*.

Chapter Fifty – Rural Northern Illinois

Shortly after Jeff and I were married, we lived in Scales Mound, Illinois. It is the highest point in the state. The town itself is quite small—two churches, two bars, and one hardware/grocery store with warped wooden floors and aisles barely wide enough for one grocery cart to go down. Quaint. We lived in Scales Mound about a year. That's not much time to gather animal stories. Nonetheless, we Carlsons had to have a few encounters.

I taught fifth grade in the town that year, with every 9- and 10-year-old kid in the twenty-one square mile district. It wasn't until after school, when all the kids had gone home, that we teachers noticed a background noise. Crickets. They were so numerous and chirped so loudly, you needed to raise your voice in order to speak to another teacher or be heard.

*****

Jeff was the student pastor of the Scales Mound Presbyterian Church, yoked with the church in the neighboring town of Apple River (which had the best tasting tap water I have ever tasted; I still dream about it). We lived in the stucco manse next to the church.

One evening close to Halloween, Jeff was working in the office in the church basement. As a newlywed, I was willingly keeping him company in the big, empty building. I could have stayed "home" next door and tried to watch something on the snowy-reception-ed 26" black and white TV, but I chose him.

A black cat casually passed by the screened office window at face level. Jeff yelled at it to go away. The cat leapt at his voice, then tore off. I like cats, but I still laughed at the jumpy scaredy-cat, not to mention that I'd jumped as well. About twenty minutes, all of a sudden that same black cat leaped at the screen, digging in its claws with all four feet. Both Jeff and I screamed, and then laughed hysterically at the cat's revenge scare.

Interesting fact: we never saw that cat again.

***

In the springtime, when calves are taken away from their mothers, there was one cow who stood just over the fence, about sixty yards from the manse, who moaned and mooed and cried all night. All. Night. You know, cows can really project their voices using their big diaphragms. You could even hear her mournful cry over the teens laying down rubber as they raced the one straight road through town.

One employee at school complained at the expense of 'having' to buy new tires for her son's car once or twice a year.

***

Just south of where we lived, and along the Mississippi River, , near Grafton, IL, bald eagles nested. This is known as "the winter home of the bald eagle." There were dozens of American Bald Eagles, flying and in their nests.

Side note: Did you also know that bald used to mean white-headed? A bald eagle has white feathers on its head. I have white hair (silver, if you please). Hey! That means I'm bald! Bald, bald, bald.

Living so near the grand Mississippi, one had to respect it. Jeff and I gotten caught on it once while canoeing. We were moving faster than we had ever paddled with no sight of people or animals. Jeff steering from the stern was the only thing keeping us from tipping. A few miles downstream we found a place to exit.

***

Besides the swift current, the river also has catfish living in it.

Catfish have always given me shivers. They're bottom feeders. Also, they have those long whiskers, frowny faces, and looks in their eyes like they know things you don't and would be afraid to know.

Then there were the stories, the stories of catfish told by locals who know the truth of these critters! I wish I would have recorded the dozen or more terrifying tales I heard at the time. From this distant perspective, there are only two I remember. You must know first, that

134

the Mississippi river is full of silt. It is muddy and brown, difficult to see your hand in front of your face even with headlights.

One story involved a jammed lock along the river. They couldn't close it to change the water level for the boats to go through. When they sent a diver down, he came face to face with a catfish stuck in the lock. A catfish twice his size. He kicked madly to the surface.

The other story involved two scuba divers working together on a lock. Two men descended. Only one man returned to the surface. His buddy was never heard of again. At this point in the tale, all the locals raised their eyebrows at each other and nodded, because *they* knew what had happened to the other diver: swallowed by a catfish!

Yes, I admit, I question the accuracy of these folk stories. But the people of the area believed them, and my eyes still water with fear whenever I think of those…those…those monstrous catfish. Or even the regular-sized.

Chapter Fifty-one – Dusky Company

While living in NY, we were a mere fifteen-minute drive west to a bridge to Canada, and a half-an-hour drive north to Niagara Falls.

There was a lovely eatery in the town of Tonawanda called Mississippi Muds. It overlooked the Niagara River. We'd go there for a rare treat of their fabulous ice cream and pleasant walk. The entire other side of the road, next to the river, lay Riverwalk Park with several playground areas scattered throughout and an amphitheater. There wasn't a sidewalk next to the busy road, but next to the river, the cement path was well used by all ages of cyclists, runners, skaters, strollers, and fishermen.

After we ordered our ice cream, we'd cross the street to walk the pathway while eating. One particular time, we'd never arrived that late in the day. Watching the sun set over the river was as much of a treat as the ice cream. We walked the path in the growing dusk. As it became darker, and no pathway lights in the parkway, people started leaving. We Carlsons continued walking, appreciating the time together as a family and the fact that there were less and less people around us.

Holding back the river were piles of large rocks. When we started, several fishermen worked their poles, sitting on those very rocks. Now, we had them to ourselves. Our boys leapt from one huge rock to another while we adults kept to the path next to them.

One of the boys spotted a black creature among the rocks. It looked like a small dog or large cat. Undoubtedly a stray. We called the boys off the rocks and told them to stay away from the animal.

We came to the end point of our walk, a small arched bridge going over a narrow runoff which led into the Niagara River. We stood on the top of the arch surveying around us. By this time, we had the park entirely to ourselves.

Something moved in my peripheral vision. I looked over the

railing, down beneath the bridge, into the gully. The bank edges and the water below us was alive with movement. Even without lights, it only took a few seconds to realize that the movement was not running water, but scrambling animals. The gully was writhing with rats, big black rats the size of cats. Hundreds of them.

We spun and ran-jogged back towards the restaurant and our car about a mile away, sitting by itself in the parking lot. We didn't keep to the path this time, for each moment more rats appeared on top of the rocky barrier immediately next to it. We ran parallel to the path, about twenty feet inland, jumping through the playground areas, keeping ever alert, at last we reached our car, leaving to the park the nighttime creatures of the Niagara River.

Chapter Fifty-two – South Dakota Miller Moth Invasion

We lived in Rapid City South Dakota during a Miller moth invasion. The small brown moths were migrating from out east, heading west to the Rocky Mountains where they would become sacrificial food for grizzly bears. The moths lingered for about two weeks in wonderful Rapid City.

I asked Jeff what he remembered of the experience. He said, "They were nasty." I asked, "What else?" He answered, "I didn't like them." I said, "More specifically." He answered, "They were messy, and smooshed powder all over the wall when you killed them."

Even though the doors and storm doors and windows were tightly sealed, the little creatures still managed to get into our house, and everyone else's. You could tell where they were hiding (sleeping) inside because of the little moth droppings going down the walls, coming from the beneath framed pictures hanging on the walls. And when you pulled back the frame, fly swatter in hand, a dozen or more flew out at your face before disappearing to other dark corners of the house.

We didn't keep our porch light on those evenings because there were so many flying around it, it didn't give off much light, anyway.

One morning on the way to work, I stopped at a red light. Of course, other cars had also stopped at the intersection. Suddenly, hundreds of moths fluttered from underneath the car and pickup truck carriages, swarming the intersection. They had obviously spent the night on the undercarriages, and when I (and others) moved our vehicles, they'd hung on for the ride until stopping.

It was a tiresome two weeks.

During our Rapid City decade, we could hike a trail for several hours, or ride over any of the hundreds of miles of narrow forest roads, enjoying the gorgeous Black Hills for the day, and then instead of paying to sleep on the hard ground in a sleeping bag in a campground with noisy, rude neighbors, we could just go home, take a shower in our own bathroom, and sleep on our own beds.

With all the advantages of not camping out, we four Carlsons backpacked one night in the Black Hills in August, 1998. We bought a second two-person backpacking tent for the ordeal. I set it up in the back yard—to make sure it had all the parts, etc.—and, wouldn't you know, a rain cloud came overhead and dumped over our little tent. I went outside to take it down and all I saw was clear blue skies, except for that one little black cloud over our house. Proof: All we Carlsons have to do is *think* about camping, and down comes the wet stuff from the sky.

When arriving at a trailhead, if there is even one other car in the lot, we look at each other, say, "It's crowded," and choose another spot to explore. Thankfully, no other vehicle was present at the start of this adventure. It was just the Carlsons and nature.

***

We started hiking along French Creek in Custer State Park where the trailhead sign warned: Keep your distance from bison. Watch for rattlesnakes and abundant poison ivy. Afternoon thunderstorms are frequent so avoid high ground. Wildfires and flash floods could occur on this trail.

We had our first aid kit with us, so after running down the warning list, felt prepared as we could enough to proceed, not that there was anything in the kit which could have helped with those.

We stopped to admire an area with ancient red rock cliffs when we realized one thing on this trail which the sign hadn't cautioned us of: Keep an eye out for biting red fire ants. While we had stopped, the little guys crawled up our legs.

The trail was called French *Creek* Trail for a reason. We crossed over the creek numerous times. Our first few crossing we were careful to find places to cross which kept us driest with rocks and logs.

We'd only hiked about an hour and done three stream crossings (no bridges) when in the middle of this knee-high grass meadow, with Peter in the lead, he stopped with his foot raised in the air. He then jumped back, shouting, "Rattle snake!!" Yep! Triangular head. Rattles on its tail. We were very lucky. And Peter was very, *very* lucky. He was close enough that he actually would have stepped on it had he placed his foot down. The coloring of the snake blended so perfectly with the dirt path that they had to keep pointing it out to me.

If you take your index finger and touch it to the tip of your thumb, that's how fat it was. We're guessing it was a younger or adolescent, because it was "only" three feet long. They can grow to eight. And Peter said he saw five rattles on it, usually one for every year, but rattles can fall off, too.

We had three choices: turn back, walk around the snake and through the grass where other snaky family members might be, or encourage it to move on.

Jeff took the lead. He rolled a couple pebbles over the snake. It didn't move. We thought perhaps it was sleeping...or dead. We were reluctant to step over it to discover the former was true. Jeff then backtracked and found a stick which he used to finally encourage the snake along. It hadn't rattled at us; probably too groggy. For all we knew, it may have stopped only two inches into the thick grass. We hustled past to the next stream crossing.

Peter got to the other side first and stood beyond this huge fallen tree which blocked the path, turned and pointed. Now touch your index fingers together and touch your thumbs together at the same time, making a circle. Move them away from each other about 2". That is how big this spider body was on the log over the creek. Long, brown, hairy legs. It was both fascinating and scary. If we hadn't just—and I mean *just—passed* the rattle snake, we would have been more shook up at this.

The following crossings there were no rocks or logs in the creek to keep us dry, so Jeff plunged on through, followed by his family. The water was only about shin-deep at the deepest, with a red rocky bottom.

We also met some bison on this trail. Literally: on the trail. We knew the story of equestrian campers who set up camp for the night on this very trail and woke to the screaming of one of the tied horses being gored by a bison. We had Band-Aids in the first aid kit, but reasonably gave the bison wide enough berth that we didn't disturb them much.

We stopped at a designated backpacking site. It had a fire pit with some logs for sitting upon which were covered with ants. There was even a wooden outhouse, which was unusable. It was surrounded by a blanket of knee-high poison ivy plants extending about twenty feet in all directions from the little shack, with the ivy crawling up the walls of the little brown house.

We saw no other hikers or campers the entire trip. We had the spot by the stream to ourselves. Nice. We sang some songs around the fire, but when I mentioned scary stories, we all quickly agreed that scary stories were fine around a campfire when there are buildings nearby or dozens of other campers within ear shot. But not out here! We were alone…as far as we could tell.

It was also a tough choice to look down at the crackling fire or up at the stars popping out without city lights to dull the scene. Every time I lifted my head there seemed to be twice the number of stars from when I'd looked before.

We left our wet hiking boots outside our two backpacking tents and said goodnight. If any bison or coyotes or snakes passed by in the dark, we didn't hear them.

There's a Far Side comic strip we always found humorous. It was of two campers in the morning. One had already put on his boots while the other was dumping from his boots a ton of snakes, spiders and insects. The caption was something like, "Henry realized too late he hadn't checked his boots before putting them on."

So in the morning, we Carlsons faithfully each checked our wet boots before putting them on. Jeff's were fine. John's were fine. Peter's were fine. Mine...were full of slugs. Why? Why, why, why? I don't know why. Maybe slugs prefer girl cooties.

Chapter Fifty-four – Black Hills Bison (and a few burro)

Our first early spring in the Black Hills we drove the hour from Rapid down to the Custer State Park paved wildlife loop. We saw bison, prairie dogs, mule deer, antelope, mountain goats, and wild burros. It felt like we were driving in a wildlife documentary.

This was our first experience with wild burros, descendants of gold miners from a century before. We didn't know what to expect. They rather blocked the road. When we stopped the van, the small herd surrounded us. When they plunged their heads through the open windows, we found it amusing, but then closed the windows. Then the burros started licking our windows. The licked all around the van. They rubbed their snotty noses, over each window. We four new-folk-to-the-area yelled, and Jeff finally moved slowly forward He cleaned the front windows with the wipers while the rest of us tried not to vomit and only look inside the van. We drove immediately to town and a car wash.

On later visits to the park, we were more comfortable. We'd take a loaf or two of end pieces of bread, exit the van, and fed them by hand. They never again licked our windows.

***

Another time down to Custer that first spring, we couldn't find any bison on the Wildlife Loop. We'd also not passed any other vehicles for about half an hour. We stopped alongside the road to take in the breathtaking view of blue skies, green pines, and red and yellow rocks in the Hills and prairie.

From the creek, about a quarter of a mile away, we noticed movement. It was dark, similar in size and shape to a bear (we knew from our Algonquin days), but it galloped, galloped in our direction. We were curious, feeling safe enough within our dark green van. Besides, if it was anything dangerous—even though we knew there were no bear in the Hills—we could speed away. It came about halfway to us before we recognized what it was: a lone bison calf. We looked around us 360 degrees. This was the only animal in sight.

It kept lopping towards us until it was twenty yards away and suddenly stopped. He turned parallel to us and stood there breathing heavily. After several minutes, it turned and sulked away. Later, I

144

figured the lost calf, seeing our dark colored van, thought we were its mama, or at least part of its herd. Poor baby.

***

One May, Jeff and I took a drive south and saw magpies (4), wild turkeys (15), mountain sheep (7), wild burros (lots) along with their furry little colts, tons of antelope, prairie dogs galore, and about 1,000 or more bison. Jeff said he'd never seen so many in one day. They were everywhere!

The domestic cows had birthed their calves by that time, and the horses and wild burros had their colts, but the buffalo cows were huge, still pregnant with their babies. They bulged, each breath seemed a struggle as they rocked back and forward. I never felt so sorry for pregnant animals before.

Later that month, Jeff and I drove back down to try to find some bison calves. We drove through the park and into Wind Cave State Park searching, but only found a couple lone males. Then I came to a dirt crossroads and asked Jeff, "which way?" because both ways eventually went back to the main road. He was so clever to have picked the right road.

We drove about a mile further down the hilly, twisting dirt road, and found about twenty-five bison. Both males and females have horns. But we knew they were female because they were in a herd, not loners like the males. We stopped. After a while, Jeff spotted a light tan calf the same color as the tall prairie grass, and then we searched

145

and found three more. A couple drove up, stopped by us and took a picture. "There are calves there," we told them. They took another photo and left in a trail of dust. We returned to our calf-search.

The longer we watched, the more calves materialized from their camouflage as they moved slightly. Before we left, we'd spotted fifteen of the little ones, fairly certain we saw all there were in that herd. We left feeling amazed with our discovery, and especially how remarkable God is to protect baby animals with perfect camouflage.

***

An early fall day I had off and Jeff didn't, I drove in our van south into Custer State Park to find some bison. Not finding any, I left the paved highway for the rocky dirt back roads. Still no allusive bison in sight. I went into neighboring Wind Cave State National Park, also winding my way through the rocky backroads, often wide enough for only one van, and too rocky and uneven ground to pull to the side if there would have been any oncoming vehicle.

The road narrowed and twisted and dipped more than a normal backroad through the parks. It was slow-going (five to seven mph). I crested a hill and began the zig-zag descent when there in the prairie valley before me was, at last, a small herd of about twenty bison. They were on either side of the road, as well as standing on it.

I slowly approached, and the bison started moving off the road. All except for a young bull, young enough to still be with the herd of cows and calves, but nearly as big as his mama. The annual Buffalo

Roundup wasn't for another couple of weeks, at which time he would be branded, vaccinated, castrated, and probably sold. But that day, there was this youngster defiantly facing me in the middle of the road.

For about two seconds, I considered backing up the eleven miles I'd come to this point to reach a paved two-lane road. But as there was nowhere to turn around anywhere on it, I'd have to drive in reverse and might not stay on the road, risking pointy quartz rocks damaging the underside of the van.

I inched the van forward. The young bull didn't move.

I was about twenty feet away when he put down his head and started pawing at the ground as if he would charge. It was only something I'd seen in movies or on TV. Once again, a calf mistook our van for an adult bison. I wasn't sure how much damage he could do, but I was sure Jeff wouldn't be too happy with any new dents by maneuvering the road in reverse while a young bull smashed into the van the whole way. I did the only other choice. I put it in neutral, revved the engine, and blasted the horn. The bull straightened up, but didn't step off the road. Soon he was back to head down position, horns pointed towards me, and pawing at the ground.

The next thing I did was undoubtedly stupid, and I'd never, ever recommend it: Battle! I stepped on the gas. My back tires spun, kicking up rocks which in turn ricocheted off of the van's undercarriage, making all kinds of racket.

The youngster straightened up, then ever so reluctantly stepped aside just as I sailed past him.

Jeff and I took an overnight trip to the Badlands of North Dakota, Theodore Roosevelt National Park, about three hours north of Rapid City.

We pulled into the parking lot of one of the visitor centers in the park. A bison herd of about fifty cows grazed ever so slowly though the area. A ranger next to his vehicle, keeping an eye on both the animals and the tourists. I went over just to be social, and was talking about our South Dakota herd when an older man approached.

"Can I put my granddaughter on the back of one for a picture?"

There have been only a very few times in my life when I have been speechless. This was one.

"No. It's too dangerous," the ranger calmly replied.

At that, the grandfather became angry and stomped off. As he left, he shouted that if the buffalo were so dangerous, why would they be allowed around people, and why weren't they fenced in? He was too distant to either receive or want an answer. I just looked at the park ranger with open mouth before returning to Jeff.

Theodore Roosevelt National Park, nearly all 70,446 acres, is indeed fenced in, with cattle guards over the road entrances. Every year people in America are gored by bison, people who don't read the numerous signs through the parks stating, "Bison are dangerous. Keep your distance." My jaw still drops every time I think of that ignorant and dangerous grandpa.

Chapter Fifty-six – Annual Buffalo Roundups

During our stay in western South Dakota twice I went to the bison roundup, a.k.a. Buffalo Roundup, at Custer State Park, a fenced-in park of 71,000 acres. People come from around the world to watch or participate in the annual roundup. (On the rare occasion it is closed to the public, most often because of fire hazards in the dry grasslands.) Both Octobers I attended alone, that is, alone with a few thousand people and 500- to 700-head of bison cows and calves. The bulls are loners and can become very aggressive.

There are no parking lots near the corrals, just the one paved road and a lot of prairie grass on the hills on each side. By getting to the site early enough, I knew I could grab a perfect viewing spot along the nine-foot tall fence where cowboys dramatically stamped the bison past the viewers. Although pickup trucks and brave cowboys on horseback roundup the herd, a helicopter earlier locates the main body of animals.

One year, I sat in my folding chair by my chosen spot at the fence with about a hundred others when a busload of middle school kids swarmed up the hill and joined us. The peaceful atmosphere exploded. They were just kids, so I don't think anyone minded their excitement. I was excited, too.

About forty-five minutes later, when the first of the herd started rounding a hill, the kids began screaming and jumping, clinging to the thin fence. I admit, it is a rather exciting moment when those first bison gallop into sight. Finally, an adult (a teacher, probably) told them to be quiet so they could hear. It took a while, but the kids settled.

For me, this is the best part of the whole weekend—when the bison suddenly appear around a far hill and the cowboys turn them between that hill and ours, funneling them into the corrals. From silent prairie valley to a thundering herd. As they pass, the ground literally vibrates from the pounding of their hooves. And this is a small herd, usually only about five hundred rounded up at once of the over one thousand in the herd. Imagine what it was like a couple hundred years ago with thousands or hundreds of thousands to a herd.

One of the years, one of the bison broke away from the herd and charged up our hill, straight towards the fence. In its panic, I have no doubt it could easily have broken through. Many visitors screamed and ran back. I remained at the fence with some others. We waved our arms and shouted. The cow jumped to a stop within five feet of me, panting and snorting, eyes wide in terror, before tossing her horned head and turning to join the rest of the herd heading towards the corrals.

Once the thrill of the stampede is over, calves are separated from the cows to get branded and vaccinated and the young males castrated (to change them into steers for meat). It gets LOUD at this point. Too loud for human speech. The bison moms are bellowing for their babes, and the scared babes are bellowing for their moms. After the calves are injected, branded and recorded, they are released to their moms. Also at this time, the herd is culled with some auctioned off to keep the large animals remaining in the park at an acceptable number. They are wild animals, but they are a managed herd.

The Buffalo Roundup is a weekend-long event with vendors hocking rancher and cowboy and Indians wears with some amazing foods. My first year, I circulated the vendors and watched the action at the corrals. The second year, after the land-vibrating thrill of the stampede, I left the bellowing animals and crowd of people to wander (by van) through the quiet park, looking for other wildlife, or to discover more bison not rounded up in the first swoop.

Chapter Fifty-seven – South Dakota Pretty Ladies

Many of the trails in the Black Hills go through Land Management land, on which ranchers can let their cattle herds graze.

Cycling downhill along a really long and straight section of the Michelson Trail, we found we couldn't allow gravity let us speed. We had to dart and weave in and out around all the cow pies lying on the gravel trail.

Another time, while hiking a trail above Roughlock Falls, Jeff and I came across a herd of cows. They were quite close to the trail, and our little hiking sticks would not do much to encourage them along even if we wanted to use them. Cows are big!

I thought I could get them moving by clapping and mooing at them. This actually worked on another trail. But all this group did was stare at me. I mooed again, but just got their big ole cow eyes staring at me.

Then, Jeff decided to try. He mooed, just once. Suddenly the meadow was alive with a near stampede as the herd charged at us.

Between my bursts of laughter, I waved my stick and shouted along with Jeff. I laughed because I figured those ladies could tell the difference between a female and a male voice, and they wanted my bull.

Chapter fifty-eight – South Dakota Roundup #1

South Dakota is divided north and south by the Missouri River. People living East River are farmers with green pastures and wear cowboy hats. People living West River are ranchers with acres of treeless prairie and wear well-used caps. While living in SD, more specifically in West River, I taught elementary school.

In one second grade classroom, nearly half the kids had a relative (often a parent) in the military. There were also Native American Indian kids. And one ranching kid. He doubled over with laughter, literally rolling on the floor, when I was explaining to a small reading group that the hamburgers we eat come from cows. Oh, what a silly, silly teacher. Tears rolled down his face as the eight-year-old laughingly tried to spit out the correct information to his teacher.

"It would be foolish to eat the *cows*," he informed me. "They make calves. We eat steers. You know…the steers are the males who have been…you know."

Yeah. I knew, but I also hadn't realized. I also knew that on that day my ranching student was the teacher.

I knew other ranchers from our church, although they didn't talk the basics with me like my eight-year-old teacher. I also knew that I wasn't going to live in South Dakota forever, so wanted to make the most of my experience in the area. I'd observed bison roundups from a distance, but really wanted to participate in an actual cattle roundup. I used the excuse that I was going to write a children's story about a South Dakota ranching kid, which I did (*Wildfire*). I ended up going to two roundups, with vaccinations and branding and all.

***

My friend Dinah is a Lakota Sioux. Her family are ranchers, or cowboy-Indians. For my first real cattle roundup I was on Dinah's family land on the Pine Ridge Indian Reservation, south of Rapid

153

City. Because I wanted to participate in the roundup, not just observe, Dinah and I went down to her parents' house the day before.

A dead calf lay near the dirt driveway area of her parent's house. I thought, how sad, and that they were waiting to bury it. But, no. Out in the pasture, a coyote had killed it, so they brought it in close to the house so that when other coyotes came to eat it in the night, they'd hear them from their house and shoot the villains who killed their livelihood.

That afternoon before the roundup, Dinah put me on an ATV for the first time in my life. I'd hoped to ride a horse, but was told ATV's are cheaper to feed. (Indian humor) I'd need to ride an ATV since we'd be using them to roundup the cattle. Driving the ATV felt like learning to ice skate. I was wobbly, slow, and unsure. I'm sure Dinah thought of me as a child as she patiently let me learn to ride the new contraption. Indian children are rarely corrected by their parents or adults. They are Wakenisha — "spirit beings." Indian parents allow their children to learn through observation and discovery. But as a white adult, I would have preferred a manual. I'm sure it took more coaching than Dinah thought, but I finally got the hang of handling the ATV before needing the machine the following morning.

Around forty people were involved that day, a real family event, with a few extras tossed in. Mostly, the women and children gathered to make food for breakfast, lunch and supper, while the men did the rounding up, separating, and branding. I felt a little guilty leaving the other women in the house to cook—that would have been another great Western South Dakota experience for many reasons—but I was interested in what went on with the animals.

I'm not sure if there was a set time in the morning for starting, but as soon as everyone arrived (at no specific cry-out of "Okay, let's go!", the women moved into the house and the men jumped back into their pickup trucks, or dove into the trunk beds, or climbed on their ATVs.

By the time I got my ATV started and remembered how to shift gears, I looked up to find all the pickup trucks and ATVs had completely vanished. Even Dinah. Some of the party apparently took off in one direction along the dirt road and had disappeared around a brown hill. I could tell by their dust, but could no longer hear the trucks. By the worn-down tire trail through the yellow-brown grass, I could tell others recently took off over the hill. I assumed that was the direction of the ATVs.

As I crested the hill, I found I'd guessed right. I saw Dinah had trailed behind the others and when she looked back to make sure I was following, she shot ahead once more. I didn't help much as far as the rounding up part went, except to point a couple stray animals toward the running herd.

We covered about fifteen miles on this roundup, getting the animals and bringing them in. I noticed government signs nailed to fence posts warning of possible unexploded bombs in the area—a remnant of WWII training on reservation land. I prayed neither running cattle nor pickup trucks sailing over mounds would set anything off. I didn't worry (too much) about an ATV running one over.

At one point when Dinah and I were stationed in a canyon to keep any strays from going back in that direction, I smelled something wretched. Dinah, true Indian that she is, observed my sniff and searched the canyon. Without me having to ask, "What is that?" Dinah found the source. "Dead coyote tossed into the ravine." I followed her eyesight. The half-eaten, decomposing body didn't make the identification any better.

With no strays backtracking, we returned to the house area and corrals. The four hundred or so cows and calves were in one large pen. Now came the separation of moms and babies part. The end result was to keep the calves in and cut out the cows who stood just outside the pen while the calves got branded and vaccinated and recorded. Dinah and I stood at the gate, only letting cows go through, but not their calves who ran after them. We also had to keep track of the number of cows which passed us.

The noise at this point was so loud that in order to be heard, you had to stand next to someone and shout into their ear. The moms were missing their babes, and the babes were missing their moms. Loud. Hundreds of moms lowing. Hundreds of babies desperately calling out. All crying loudly for each other. Loudly. At this point, humans communicated more by sign than by speech.

Once the animals were separated, the guys dug a three-foot diameter pit right in the dirt of the pen and built a fire in it. Into this went three iron brands, for although they were one family, they were three sets within that family. Each mom and calf had ear tags with the same numbers to identify who belonged to whom, both bovine and human wise.

One man would grab a bellowing calf and take it to two seated people who held the legs and neck to keep the calf steady while getting branded. The person holding the backend legs needed to make sure the calf's tail was pressed against the butt with one boot so the calf's green diarrhea poo wouldn't shoot over them. I mostly got the tail-end job. As soon as the branding and vaccinating was done, and castration if it was male, the calf was released and another brought over.

Other people separated the branded calves and allowed them back out into the pasture with their mothers. As the morning went on and the moms and babes were once more united, the noise level constantly lowered.

I would like to add here that although branding does hurt the calf, it is only for a short time. It is necessary for identification. For cattle rustling is a very real thing for modern day ranchers just as it was in the past. Ranching is a business and each animal must be accounted for. It is the people's livelihood, and is our food.

***

Back in civilization at church I told a rancher my age how I helped with the roundup on the Rez by riding an ATV. He turned up his nose (probably with prejudices both of Indians in general and of a

157

woman doing a man's job). He told me how rounding cattle up with an ATV would never work because the noise would scare and scatter them. Horses, he informed me, were the only way to bring in cattle for a roundup. I'm guessing that was his experience, but given my weekend, ATVs had obviously worked. Even the bison roundup used pickup trucks as well as horses, Mr. Cowboy-man.

Chapter Fifty-nine – South Dakota Roundup #2

My second South Dakota roundup was with a non-Indian family living east of Rapid City with about three hundred head of cattle. Again, it was a family event. This time, I was the only outsider. Again, the women stayed indoors doing food preparations while the men did the roundup and branding and vaccinating. These gender-specific jobs are still alive and well out west, but my friend Kodi worked the roundup with me because she was kind, and wanted to show this city-slicker the way they did it.

Kodi's family lived in three different houses on the ranch while Kodi and her husband lived in town. On the roundup were three brothers, Kodi's dad, Kodi and me. Kodi and I were in one pickup, two men in another, and two went on horseback. The herd grazed together past the creek on a hill about two miles away. There were trees near the creek, as is true of most Western SD water sources, with the rest of the ranch pasture land. The two trucks minded the sides of the herd from about fifty yards away, while the two on horseback got them moving from behind slowly walking towards the house and corrals.

The creek crossing was a bottleneck between the trees, with no bridge. It was wide enough for one or two pickup trucks side by side, or five to seven cattle crossing at a time. Kodi and I stayed near the creek to make sure there were no stragglers. I got out of the truck to hike down the creek bed to get some photos. While I was alone, I heard a rustle behind me. I turned to see a lone cow coming at me, trotting away from the rest of the obedient herd. I waved my hands at the lost beast and said, "HA!" and then shouted for Kodi in the pickup back by the crossing. By the time Kodi realized what I was shouting about, I had that lone bovine trotting back with her "people."

Kodi's father was awesome. After he realized I wasn't there to be an anti-branding person, he took me under his wing and made sure I experienced all I could know about Roundup Day.

(A side note concerning branding. One story a friend told me was how a police friend of his stopped a carload of young men "acting suspicious." This wasn't profiling this time, because the policeman heard a noise coming from the truck. He first thought it was a human, but no. It was a stolen calf, who was then returned to the rightful ranch because of the brand.)

It doesn't matter which ranch, which cattle, the same loud-loud mooing sounded as the cows and calves got separated.

One cow charged up a wrong chute and got separated from the others, dead-ending in a different pen. I stood by the gate so she wouldn't go back to the field. I expected her to stop when she saw the closed-but-not-latched gate. Cows must be smart. It charged right at me, anyway, slamming her huge body into the gate. I had stepped back, so when the distance quickly closed between the metal gate rail and my forehead, I saw stars for the first time in my life. Kodi's dad asked if I wanted to go into the house. I'm not sure if he wanted me out of the way or wanted to keep me safe. My goose egg and I chose to stay.

This time, instead of taking three people to brand a calf, it only took one. Kodi's family had a calf branding table. A calf was ushered through a chute and between two horizontal "tables." Once the calf was in place, the tables gently pushed against each side of the calf and then flipped the animal sideways where the brander could mark his herd, vaccinate the calf, then straighten up the tables and release the animal. It was simple, slick, and quick. Also, there was no fire pit. The branding iron was kept in a waist-high metal cooker similar to a BBQ grill.

Kodi's dad told me that if I wanted to experience this rather than just observe, I would have to both brand and vaccinate a calf. On the other roundup day, I hadn't done either of those.

I knew my instinct would be to pull away once the calf realized there was some burning going on. So I observed as he branded, and counted. The calves were quiet and calm as they were turned sideways. Once the branding iron hit the fur and skin and smoke got into your eyes and nostrils, it took three seconds before the calf bleated out. Another really, really long second and the brand was complete. Once the calf turned hoof end down and was released from the table, she tore down the opposite chute for her mama, no longer bleated. I found it amazing how each cow and calf found each other so quickly. Also amazing was that burnt hair smell lingered in your nostril hairs for several days after.

I was more nervous about handling the huge vaccination needle. Again I observed first, and then wrapped my hand around that thing and punctured and pressed in the medicine.

I'm glad for the roundup experiences, and I'm sure I would do it again given the opportunity, but at the moment I'm glad someone else has those jobs. I do like beef.

Chapter Sixty – Birds, Birds Everywhere

While single and living in Wisconsin, I tried to condition myself for my first backpacking trip by taking country walks with my filled backpack. I was living in a house in Merrimack along the Wisconsin River. I was the only "year-round resident" among several nearby summer cottages.

Off I tramped with my backpack strapped to my back, down

the country road, until someone let me know he was stronger than this first-time backpacker—a red-winged blackbird whose territory I'd walked too near. It screamed and dove at me repeatedly like something out of Hitchcock's "The Birds." I turned back home.

Red-winged blackbird: 1. Road-hiking Sandy: 0.

***

Once we Carlsons Four canoed between Pog Lake and Lake of Two Rivers when we stopped paddling at the sound of an approaching loon. It flew around the river's wood-lined bend, and about five feet above the river, right over our heads and out of sight around the bend behind us.

One year there was a mating pair of loons on Pog Lake, where we camped. It was grand to have them part of our daily natural sight and sound experience during those six August days.

***

In South Dakota, birds in the wild became even more interesting. There were bald eagles, golden eagles, turkeys, falcons, hawks, and dozens of smaller fowl.

One of our first days driving in the Black Hills, I was at the wheel. Suddenly Jeff started pointing and saying, "Big bird! Big bird!" An eagle had flown within a few feet of our car and perched in a tree. It was so thrilling to have one so close that Jeff couldn't think of the bird's name. It was a big bird.

Another time in the Hills, we drove past a red rock cliff which bordered the curvy road. The cliff top was about forty feet above the road. Suddenly several very large animals started falling down around us. I thought it was the Apocalypse. Nope. It was a flock of turkey, about twenty-five of them, going from the cliff edge on our left to the shoulder across the road on our right. Some of those very large birds nearly smacked into our little car. I didn't know turkeys flew, and perhaps they don't. It was more like a quickly descending parachute jump.

On the other side of the road was a small cornfield. Once land-bound again, the intelligent birds scrambled off to seek their free meal in the cornfield.

In Michigan, we filled our birdfeeder once a week, year-round. Jeff kept a pair of binoculars and two bird books next to his chair in the living room for identifying the dozens of fowl species visiting.

Then came the storm of 2011.

Memorial Weekend Monday of 2011, we had 110 mph sheer force winds come through our wooded neighborhood. I could barely hear the siren even after Jeff told me about it. Usually I was the one who first heard the sirens. We went faithfully into the basement. A couple of minutes later, there was the sound of a banshee rushing down our chimney accompanied by cinder-block-moving crashes and thuds. Within three minutes the winds had stopped. When we ventured upstairs, we couldn't see outside our windows because leaves were plastered against them. Opening the front door, we saw our house and yard and neighborhood was piled with fallen trees. Two of our one-hundred-year-old oaks had gone through our house.

The view of the sky in our yard changed from only seeing 10% of it in our previously wooded neighborhood, to being able to see 95% of sky. In just a few moments of wind, our neighborhood changed from a thick woodland forest into a prairie. People came from all over the nation to come help clear this area.

Our little two-lane road with no shoulders or sidewalks was lined with work trucks down both sides of the street. Every yard had a dumpster in it. If someone wanted to get by on the road and met facing traffic, one of the two vehicles would have to back up. And there were chainsaws and trucks beeping backwards from dawn 6:30 AM until dusk till too dark to see at 9 PM, every day for three months. We had no electricity for the first week.

Chapter Sixty-one – 2011 Storm Effect on Animals

The storm also affected our neighborhood animals. We especially noticed we no longer had the variety of birds visiting our feeder. Instead, there was a flock of sparrows who, without other competition, ate the entire seed in the feeder in half a day.

A grackle found its way to our feeder, only eating what the sparrows dropped to the ground. I shall never forget that grackle's eyes—wide, white, crazed. They were in such contrast to his shiny sunlit-reflected black-green feathers. This bird had survived the storm, but the survivor's eyes were different from any bird I have seen before or since.

A hawk family—two parents and two chicks—also survived in a tree across the street. The chicks were too young to fly or swim off like the swans and geese had done with their chicks, so they remained in the neighborhood with the sounds of hundreds of saws blaring from dawn to dusk for three months.

After four years about half a dozen bird species other than sparrows began to return to our backyard feeder. I imagine that when the young trees we planted post-storm finally mature in a decade or two, this house will once more have a large variety of fowl flying around it.

***

Neighbors a few houses down from us had seven golden retriever dogs as rescue animals. They complained to me about how expensive the medicine was to calm down their dogs during this three months' time. All of the dogs were nervous from the fifteen hours a day of chainsaws, and multiple other kinds of saws going on those three months. I related to the poor dogs.

When a large, old oak tree on our property fell, ants moved from there (hollow at the bottom) into our house. Lots of ants. But, take away their food, and ants go marching on.

I saw no raccoons in our neighborhood for years following the storm. Any homes in trees were annihilated. Of course, deer stayed away from the noise at that time, too. I wished I could have.

Chapter Sixty-two – Bee Powerful

In the mid-1980's we Carlsons lived in the three-bedroom manse next to the church in Cheektowaga, NY. Either the first or second summer, I noticed bees coming into our house, especially in Peter's room. Several were inside his closet, where there was access to the attic through the ceiling.

I got a ladder and peered into the darkness. It sure looked like there were bees flying around on the far side up there. I found our mosquito netting hats and put one on to take a closer look. But the netting made it too dark to see much. Halfway across the unfinished attic, I determined there were a great many bees up there. I'd heard of bees making hives in house walls and coming into the house through electrical outlets, so decided to tell the church to call for an exterminator.

The exterminator guy came, merely poked his head through

the access hole to the attic and hurried back down the ladder, frightened by what he'd seen. He fumigated. Peter slept in John's room for the next few days. And the bees died. I wondered at my bravery of crawling so near the hive when the experienced exterminator wouldn't…or was it stupidity or ignorance?

* * *

When the solar eclipse of September 2017 happened, we in Michigan were not in the total eclipse path, but knew the sun would be partially covered from our location. Realizing it's a bad thing to look directly at the sun at any time, when it started getting dark outside that day (not quite dusk-like, and about fifteen minutes before the darkest it would get here), I decided to sit on our front porch to horizontally watch the eclipse affect as our neighborhood darkened.

Earlier that summer, bees built a hive under our porch. I'd often sat out on the bench, watching their busy goings to and fro. They'd never bothered me. But right then, at the height of the eclipse for our area, three of the little guys came over and stung me!

This got me thinking about power. Actual or not, I figured the hive thought I was the one causing the disruption of their daylight. In other words, they assumed I had the power to block out the sun throughout the neighborhood. It was an assumption, or rather a misassumption, but one they acted upon. I felt their response in actual power—by their stings. And for the following couple of days their power continued over me with the pain from those stings, followed by a week of itching.

167

The first time I saw a bear in the wild was when I worked at Yellowstone National Park as a group of us hiked past it. That bear was a grizzly. Welcome to the world of bears. I learned to wear "bear scare" bells around my ankles as I hiked to warn of my coming.

Between my freshman and sophomore years of college (summer of 1969, and the summer when man first stepped onto the moon), I participated in the first year of the Campus Crusade ministry of placement of college kids in National Parks. I was assigned to Mammoth Hot Springs in Yellowstone National Park. Because this program was new, there was only one other Campus Crusade person in the park, and he was fifty miles away.

To get to Yellowstone from Ohio, my mom drove me in our car to the Hopkins International Airport. From there, I took a plane, a train, a taxi, and a bus as well as spent my first night alone in a motel.

I'd never seen mountains before this time. So, for the first two weeks I felt like I was walking around inside a postcard. I also discovered it was very difficult for a flatlander like me to breathe at that altitude.

I was hired by Yellowstone Park Company as a hotel maid. Maids worked in pairs to make the beds and clean the rooms. We were preceded to each room by a college boy who stripped the beds, emptied the trash, then followed after us to vacuum and spray Lysol.

After a couple of days, an opportunity came up where they needed a maid to work out in the cabins area. I leapt at the chance to be outside versus stuck in a stuffy, ancient hotel building. All. Day. Long.

Working the cabins not only had the gorgeous mountain views for 360 degrees, but there were also animals to keep us company. Throughout the eighty cabins area were holes made by groundhogs, small rodents, cousins to prairie dogs. While we worked in one cabin, a neighborhood of groundhogs might come out to in front of the cabins to feed or sunbathe. Then as my partner, Suzie, and I emerged from a finished cabin, they'd scramble for their holes. Many of the holes were dug at the bases of the cabins. When they escaped to their homes, they'd strike their heads against the wood. *Thud-thud-thump*. I thought they were very stupid creatures.

Once in a while a bear or even bear family would wander into the cabin area. Knowing this, we were always cautious about opening the doors when we left a cabin. We didn't want to startle it. When we did spot one of the burly critters, we would just sit back and hole up in the cabin for a few minutes until it wandered away, after which we then made a dash to the next cabin to continue cleaning.

***

We got one day off work every seven to eight days. Hitchhiking was popular and accepted at this time. It was the only way most of the car-less college staff got to visit various places in the park on our days off. We normally didn't have any trouble getting rides.

We held out a sign reading "Park Employees" and were readily picked up. Usually. I felt inclined to tell our rides what I knew about the park. I enjoyed it so much that I considered being a tour guide. There was so much to learn and to share with others. But I never considered that a "real" job.

One of my days off, a fellow female employee and I hitchhiked one hundred miles south to the Tetons. There, we drank a glass of water at a closed ski resort, then turned to return north to Mammoth Hot Springs where we worked.

About half-way back towards our dorms, our ride was turning west at a very busy four-stop-sign intersection, while we wanted to continue north. We thanked them, got out of the car, crossed the intersection, and held out our sign. About the same time, a black bear joined us at the intersection. As usual, whenever there was a bear sighting, cars stopped. Lots of cars stopped. Some people tossed out food to the bear. There was so much traffic, but they were more interested in taking pictures of a real live bear than picking up two hitchhikers standing nearby.

Knowing we were the only humans outside of vehicles, we two slowly inched our way backwards, further from the bear, further from the intersection where we would be more likely to be seen. Still no one picked us up. Finally, all the cars dispersed and we two college girls were left alone with one big bear lumbering a few yards from us. We continued to walk backwards. I wanted to keep my eye on every movement of the creature.

Suddenly, from very close behind us, came a noise. We screamed and jumped with a twist, expecting to be surrounded by bear. Instead, the noise was from a piece of litter rustling across the road. We quickly turned back to the intersection. The bear had fled—perhaps because of our screams. Then again, maybe it was a sneaky bear, a bear which was tip-toeing through the cover of the woods, circling around to reach tasty-young-college-girls-us.

It was several minutes (which felt like hours) before a lone car pulled up to the intersection and turned towards us, aiming in our direction. I stood in the middle of the road and waved my arms to flag it down. The choice was simple: get run over by a car or eaten alive by a bear. Luckily, they stopped, and after hearing our story, and undoubtedly confirming it by our sheet-white faces and trembling, they agreed to give us a lift. Lucky us. In fact, they were going all the way north to Mammoth where we worked.

Chapter Sixty-four – Sunset in Yellowstone

One day off, I happened to have the same day off as Randy, our cabin boy who went before and after us maids. We decided to hike a nearby mountain. He was from Illinois and I from Ohio, neither having been in mountains before that summer. He wanted to watch sunset from a mountaintop. We hitched a ride the five miles up to the trailhead (with no parking spots) and started hiking.

Each step during that two-hour mountain hike up was

stunningly gorgeous. I remember feeling disappointed when we reached the top and we could no longer go further up. We sat on the mountaintop, ate our employees-boxed suppers, and watched the sun go down over a distant mountain.

Did I mention that neither of us had been in the mountains before? It struck both of us at the same time that while we were still sitting high in sunlight, the valleys below us were now shrouded in darkness. We weren't certain whether we would even be able to see the trail back, especially since neither of us had brought a flashlight. We employees had heard stories of tourists getting lost in Yellowstone while hiking off trail and walking down the wrong side of the mountain. So, besides the woods getting dark around us, there was also the real possibility of getting lost.

And then we heard it. One lone howl. A wolf? A coyote? We figured one animal was manageable, but we'd have to keep a vigilant watch on our way through the darkness, for both the true trail and for yellow eyes watching us in the dark.

Then we heard another howl. We collected our things started moving. Quickly.

A third and fourth howl.

It no longer mattered to us if what we heard were wolves or coyotes. Whichever they were, there was a pack of them. And they were near. More howls sounded. Were they from the same ones or more joining the pack? My companion picked up some rocks to throw at them. I knew I was a lousy aim, and didn't imagine that a few tossed rocks would matter much against a pack, but I put some rocks into my pockets anyway.

There had been no dusk. It was sunlight, and then dark. As howls continued, we ran down the mountainside. Part of me was glad we didn't have flashlights to confirm any fellow beings.

We were both nearly tripped when we burst onto the flat, smooth, black road. With no streetlights, and no car head lights to let us know where we were, one moment we were stumbling over roots and rocks in a dark wood, and the next were on level, dark pavement. We'd made it down in an amazingly short amount of time, about half the time it took us to climb up. We couldn't see Mammoth Village lights because of the curve in the road. We doubted any tourists would be traveling this late in the day. They were either eating at a park restaurant or settling into their rooms. The creatures of the night still howled about us.

We continued at a run down the middle of the road when we heard a car approaching from behind. We stood to the side of the road and waved our arms as the headlights hit us. The car nearly veered off the road when it saw us before it slowed, and then came to a stop.

We jumped into the welcoming car which nearly blinded us by the interior lighting, and hysterically poured out our adventure to our saviors who then returned us safely to our dormitories.

One time visiting my grandparents', Roger and Bette and I discovered the corn bin was unlocked. That was a first. In the past, we could only see between the slats of the walls to the dried corn within. But that day it was free for us to not only peek inside, but to enter the forbidden territory.

Inside, we discovered not only a pile of the dried corn but a machine which stripped the kernels off of the ears. The machine stood about waist high. To make it work, you put the corn cobs into a top shoot, turned the handle and the kernels came out down a metal slide where obviously you would have placed a bucket to catch them. We saw no bucket in the shed.

There were two jobs and three kids. Being the oldest, Roger decided he would put in the corn and turn the handle. Being the next oldest, I was going to catch the kernels in my hands. Meanwhile, poor Little Bette stood outside the door of the crib, pouting.

I knelt at the base of the machine and held out my cupped hands anticipating the corn kernels to come down the slide. Bette grumbled because she could not see from her position.

At first nothing happened. Roger cranked harder. And then a few kernels began to tumble down. I smiled. And then something else tumbled out right into my hands. It took me a second to realize what it was. A mouse. I screamed and threw the fat grey critter over my head and out the door and ran from the crib. Roger and Bette followed after, trying to find out what happened. They hadn't even seen the mouse, which had only momentarily been on my palms, but knew it had to be true because of my reaction.

***

For a science experiment my junior year of high school, I decided to show what happens in a population explosion. I bought two white mice—one male and one female. I kept them in a glass aquarium behind the door of my bedroom. It wasn't long before eight cute, pink and blind mouselets were born. In a couple of weeks, they grew up nice and white and furry when, lo and behold, just three weeks after they were born, there were additional cute, pink and blind mouselets in the aquarium. By the time my science experiment was completed and my report written, there were a couple hundred white mice then in three cages in the basement workshop, some escaping the high glass walls much to the delight of my cat, and with cannibalism going on, and the grandpa of all of them mating with the youngest ones. Gross-gross-gross. I remember giggling when I did my oral presentation, because that's what I used to do when I was scared or completely disgusted, but there was nothing at all funny about my population results.

I believe I was at theatre after school the day when my mother and sister took them someplace to be eliminated. I wish we would have thought to take them to a zoo instead. Bette was most traumatized

175

by the car ride as she was in the backseat with the three aquariums, continually pushing the furry little mice down from climbing over each other to escape.

***

Shortly after we were married, Jeff and I traveled from Illinois to Ohio to visit my parents. They lived in a house on three acres of land across from the wooded Cuyahoga County Park system. We slept on the pull-out couch on the enclosed porch, where my dad normally sat to watch TV. He'd often snack on many things, including Hershey's © kisses in their little wrapped foils.

Our first night there, we were kept awake by the sound of crinkling aluminum foil. We assumed it had to be mice searching through the candy wrappers. The following morning, I cleaned the room of any food while my mom set out three mouse traps. As soon as the others left the room that night, Jeff and I heard, "Snap. Snap. Snap."

Mom came and took care of the captured rodents. We were correct. Mice.

After fourteen more mice had been captured and it was quite for a while, Jeff and I settled down for our second night's "sleep." We didn't tell Mom about the three additional "snaps" until morning.

176

For about a week I once owned a pet mouse.

Part of the time I was teaching, I lived in a small cabin in Wisconsin Dells, part of a motel grouping. I first noticed the mouse droppings in my itty-bitty kitchen area near the stove. Then, I discovered a cereal box had a hole chewed near the bottom. It was late fall. The hungry little guy was trying to find someplace warm for the winter.

Figuring it was a mouse, and figuring that it liked that kind of cereal, each morning before work I left the critter a lid-full. I figured if I controlled what it ate, it would leave the rest of my food alone. Each evening when I'd return home from work, the lid would be empty of food. He even popped into view a few times with his dark, beady eyes and twitching whiskers. I'm sure he was thanking me. Until...I found it had made its nest on the lower part of the oven which I obviously did not use very often.

As I told my dilemma to a friend, he became shocked that I was feeding a mouse in my house. I explained it was very cute and that we had this relationship. He emphatically told me I could not use my oven. I countered that I could use the burners on the top of the stove. But when he added that mice are notorious for chewing electrical wires in houses, fraying them, and starting fires, I became as seriously concerned as he was. After all, I didn't want all my possessions to burn down in the middle of the night. Nor me.

The next day this betrayer bought d-con © mouse poison and added it to the food in the lid. The little guy took it all. The following day, I left more food mixed with poison, but the first lot had obviously done the job. I never saw those cute little whiskers again.

Chapter Sixty-seven – Children's Garden Mice

One year I worked at a children's garden in Battle Creek. The previous children's director had left a bunch of seeds and flower bulbs in the shed near the garage which was the storage area for all of the children's garden projects. Unfortunately, the seeds and bulbs were put in plastic bags. Therefore, mice from the area came to feast in their little castle eatery. Every single day when I opened the door, I was not only nearly knocked out from the smell, but dozens of mice would scatter along the shelves and floor. I knew that even though I had to get something from a shelf in there that those mice had not left the building. They were still there, watching my every move, lurking behind different pots, paints, brush pans, pinecones, etc., just watching-watching-watching me, anxious for me to leave so they could get on with their feasts and making more babies.

I immediately removed all of the bulbs and seeds, but it seemed those little mice did not want to leave their winter home. The pink insulation of the heater and refrigerator made their nests so soft.

The other staff did not believe me when I told them of the amount of mice in the shed. Finally, one brave female employee who didn't mind capturing mice set out five traps. The next day there were five trapped mice. She resent them and the next day five more were caught. But the third day, three of the traps had snapped, but there were no mice in them, and the food was gone. The fourth day, all food in the mousetraps had vanished, and only some of the traps snapped shut, but not a single mouse had been caught. Tricky-clever mice.

My fellow employee didn't want to use poison, so she set out five mouse-sized bags with sticky paper inside. The next day five more mice flopped around, alive, stuck to the sticky paper in the bags. She removed them. The next day only one bag had trapped a mouse. Mice sure are fast learners!

In the meantime, the mice had discovered more seeds which I'd stored in thick plastic gallon containers. Those determined rodents chewed a mouse-sized door into the bottom side of the containers. I put what seeds the mice had left into metal containers. Ha! They couldn't get at it now, but they still wouldn't leave their home.

Since I still refused to touch the dead or trapped living mice, the other employee got tired of removing the critters every single morning. She finally gave in to her last-resort tactic: d-con © mice poison.

After she set out the poison, the mice population seemed to become more manageable, but there were still many of them around—as witnessed by the tiny black bullet droplets they'd leave behind. One day I ordered fifty tree seedlings to give out to children coming to the Garden later that week. Naturally, I stored them in the Garden store room, a.k.a., the work shed. A couple of days later it became quite warm, so I went to check on the plants to make sure they weren't wilting. Walking in, I noticed the seedlings I'd left on the shelves and work table had been nibbled down to the soil. There were a few plants left on boards of 2" x 4" straddling some five-gallon plastic buckets. Inside each bucket was two or three dead seedling-eating culprits. I actually felt sorry for the mice this time. I wasn't sure whether they'd died from eating that particular tree-plant, or if they couldn't jump out of the bucket once they'd fallen inside, or maybe they'd developed heat stroke. It didn't really matter. More dead mice. Yay! No more tree-seedling-mouse-traps available.

Chapter Sixty-eight – Red Worms

While in South Dakota, my back-door neighbor, Nancy, got some red worms from a friend. Soon after, she had to leave town for a week. As her husband was blind and her three kids were in college, I was a logical choice to watch her worms. Besides, I volunteered.

She got the red worms (v.s. earth worms, mind you) because they turn garbage into fine soil for the garden. Nancy and I were both avid gardeners, and fully aware of the benefits of worms. I've tried for years to get Jeff to let me have some red worms, but I'd been voted down each time. I figured that I *had* to watch Nancy's worms since there was no one else to do it. Also in the back of my mind was that maybe Jeff would see that it wasn't so bad a venture after all.

Red worms will freeze, so need to stay where it's warm. In a large Rubber-Maid tub with 1" holes placed every 2-3" apart, I put a bedding of moist shredded newspaper on the bottom. On top of that was a thin layer of dirt. Atop the dirt, I placed a few plant remains (lettuce hearts, carrot peels, etc.). All topped with another layer of shredded moist newspaper. It can't be too wet. Can't be too warm. Can't be too cold. Can't have too much garbage (or it stinks). Must have no light. But other than that, all rather low-maintenance.

I wrote on the calendar reminding me to check the worms every other day (for food and moisture). I told Nancy if I wrote it small maybe Jeff wouldn't notice. Nancy said she could write anything she wanted on their calendar. Her husband couldn't see anything!

Jeff's view of the worm-sitting business was out of sight, out of mind: "I don't want to hear about them. I don't want to see them. But if a single one escapes, your pillow will be stuffed with worms!"

Our boys were in high school at the time. John was my first "victim." He was concerned they would escape from the holes which were twice as round as the worm circumferences. It seemed a legitimate concern. I tried to assure him they had a moist home. They had their darkness. They had their food. Whyever would they want to leave their nice little home?

All of their lives I tried to get our boys interested in things outside their normal range of interests, so I nearly had to bribe Peter to look at the red worms I was "sitting." After five days passed, and the worms would soon be gone, he finally agreed. When I started walking into the utility room, every muscle in his body wiggled. "IN THE HOUSE!! YOU'RE KEEPING THEM IN THE HOUSE!!" He never did make it over to see the worms. I think it upset him most because they only had five steps to climb to reach his nearby bedroom. We other family members were safe by an additional fourteen steps to reach our two bedrooms in the split-level house.

I was a little disappointed in the worms. After the first week, they didn't finish the half banana peel I gave them, nor even the large lettuce leaf. However, they were nibbled at. What did I expect? Overnight soil? It takes time even for worms to poop! The night before Nancy returned home, I was able to see a bunch of worm babies with a flashlight.

The following year, I made my own worm bin. My guys were not very pleased they were permanent animals v.s. guests, so I took them to school. My fifth graders liked the care-responsibility. One student even named them, although I'm pretty sure he couldn't really tell them apart. Pretty sure. When we moved to Michigan, I had to bid a sad farewell to my little buddies.

I'm an early bird; my husband's a night owl. We've learned to work around our personal clocks. The spring of the first year we were married (1979), we took a week's trip to state parks around Wisconsin. One night, we camped at Merrick State Park along the Mississippi River. I was awakened in the morning by what sounded like a cat stuck in the tree above us. The more I listened, the more I was certain it was a bird.

I got dressed, grabbed the binoculars and bird book, and deserted my sleeping husband. Only one other person in the campground was awake, and he was several sites away. I sat at our picnic table and located the bird crying so uniquely and pitifully from the tree overhanging our tent. I looked it up in the book. It was a cat bird. Well named!

I looked back through the binoculars in order to confirm the markings, following the trunk up towards the nest, and noticed movement. About two thirds of the way up, a snake was climbing over the bark of the tree. Who knew? I'd always known snakes as ground creatures. Then I recalled that snakes ate eggs. No wonder the cat bird cried so. I could have thrown a rock to knock the snake off the tree, but it would then be on the ground at my feet. Besides, there was always the next time for the snake to make another egg-snatching attempt when I wasn't there to be guardian of the eggs. I decided not to watch that horror unfold and took a walk down to the Mississippi River.

A narrow trail went out through chest-high grass and over mushy, swampy ground to the point extending into the river. It wasn't a long trail, only about one hundred yards. I imagined that fishermen used this trail. I watched the beautiful sunrise-lit bluff on the western side and occasionally stretched up on my tip-toes to try to catch a glimpse of the river. I let my feet judge when the soggy ground would become too wet to support me. I was nearing my goal and my hiking boots were sinking in deeper—a couple inches, three inches—into uncertain ground. I stopped. I didn't want to sink up to my knees in muck and be unable to get out with no one knowing where I was so early in the morning. I sadly acknowledged I wouldn't reach the edge of the river, and that the river flowed under the tentative ground upon which I stood. I remained still in the soft earth for a quiet moment, reflecting on God's glory of the early morning, of the quiet, of water all around me, being both a part of water and land.

Then, for the first time of the soggy morning hike, instead of looking up, I looked down. At my feet, and stretched across and all along as far as I could make out through the curved grass trail, were brown snakes with thick diameters of two inches. Hundreds of them. And those were only the ones I could see crisscrossing the narrow trail. What about in the grassy marsh to my left and right?

I did a high-stepping sploshy run back to the campsite, only occasionally looking down to try to not step on a snake—an impossible task. And how many had I squished into the muck getting to my turnaround point? I bolted up the dry hill to our campsite and sat cross-legged on the picnic table until Jeff finally woke up.

Finding out that snakes climbed trees had been difficult enough to swallow. Discovering from a park ranger later that day that these are harmless bullsnakes didn't calm my heart much. Imprinted in my mind for a thousand years to come was the image of hundreds of large slithering brown snakes, blocking my way to non-snake safety.

Chapter Seventy – Salted Nuts

You would think that I learn certain lessons. You would think.

I still don't like bright lights at night. So, thirty some years after being married to Jeff, I wanted to have a night snack and didn't turn on any lights. I reached into the pantry for some mixed nuts. I opened the can and grabbed a small handful, placing them into my mouth.

Being in the dark, I must have missed my mouth, because I felt the salt on my cheeks. I brushed it off and reached for another few nuts. Suddenly, things started moving inside my mouth, around my lips, and over my hands. Whatever it was, I knew it wasn't nuts.

Click!

I flicked on the kitchen light to discover a straight line of ants going from the ceiling of the pantry, down the wall, over the shelf, and into my can of nuts… and consequently, into my mouth.

Chapter Seventy-one – Murder!

Twice now (in fourteen years) we have had a murder of crows in our Michigan neighborhood. The first time was amazing, and also a little creepy. Thousands of black birds sat in the November bare-leafed oaks, with hundreds more flying about. The first time they came, I was so impressed, I went outside and danced on the lawn with them singing (caw-ing) to me from the sky.

After a couple of days, though, their caw-ing became a little irritating, especially when they started up before dawn. Thousands of caw-ing crows. It was loud.

During the mid-day hours, they were eerily quiet, still seen roosting in the trees. But we still had to walk the seventy steps outside to our mailbox. Sometimes they would silently watch. That was disturbing. Sometimes one would start up the cry of intruder and hundreds other join in while others flew about. A couple of times when they were silently watching me, I would clap my hands together, and the murder would start up their loud cries in flight.

The aftermath of a murder is quite messy, even with a murder of crows. Our driveways and roads and yards were full of white splotches (droppings), and small twigs lay everywhere. You couldn't take a step without crunching some of their tossed-to-the-ground sticks.

Murder! Caw.

Chapter Seventy-two – Deer hunting with the Carlson Men

Besides just spotting deer live in Wisconsin, there was hunting season. My first November in Wisconsin was eye-opening for big-city gal me. In fact, when I moved to Wisconsin for my first teaching job, I thought I was going into the northern wilderness. Not raised with fishermen nor hunters, this was new territory for me.

Hunting season in Wisconsin involves seeing dead deer strapped to hoods or trunks of cars or antlers sticking out the beds of pickup trucks. Deer season. Everyone I knew who hunted did so to feed their family for the year on venison. Whoever shot an animal, would share it equally with the entire group of hunters even if no one else killed any.

My first year married I wanted to try deer hunting with the Carlson men. My father-in-law was concerned with my red down coat because it had white and grey fox fur around the hood, meaning it looked like the tale of a Whitetail deer. He wisely made me tuck it in.

We drove out before dawn to a privately owned wooded area where they had permission to hunt for that week starting Thanksgiving weekend.

In the dark woods, Jeff placed me in a spot by myself, and then walked out of sight. I had imagined we would stay together, but it's a good thing we didn't because I probably would've talked to him the whole time. That would have gotten him very angry.

So, I sat there alone on the side of a hill with my back against a tree trying to keep my hands warm in the single-digit temperature. There was no snow, but it was Wisconsin-cold. And as a hunter, it would never do to move about to get my blood circulation going to stay warm. Did I mention it was cold?

It's interesting how your imagination can play with you when you are alone in the woods after several hours. I caught movement in my peripheral vision but when I looked, there were no squirrels or small critters nearby. No crinkling of dried leaves. No snapping of twigs. Just periodic "glimpses" from my sides. It was as though the woods held small elves or fairies who would freeze when I turned and camouflaged themselves perfectly into the woodland rather than be discovered.

I only went deer hunting that one day that the whole weekend. I also was the only one in the party of eight to see any deer. I saw a wounded doe limp past, about twenty-five yards in front of me. It was a sideways shot. I'd been in rifle club in high school. I was a pretty good shot. I knew I could have struck and killed her, but thought maybe another hunter, the one who'd hit her, was following her trail. I let her go. Besides, I didn't have the doe tag. Anyone registered hunter could shoot a buck, but there was only one doe tag allowed per group. At lunchtime my father-in-law told me I should have shot the deer even though I did not have the doe tag, and later get the doe tag from whoever in the group had it. I didn't know the "rules."

Also that morning, sitting with my back against a tree, failing to keep my hands warm, I heard a quiet noise rustle the leaves behind me. I held my breath. There were slow, calculated footsteps. This was no squirrel nor wood elf. It wasn't until the sound was nearly upon me, about five feet away, that I slowly turned my head. In true deer form, a doe was leading the way with her buck following after. Just that slight turn of my head was enough to startle the doe, who then startled the buck. As they galloped back away up and over the hill, I knew I could have hit the doe, anyway, but only in her backside. It wouldn't have been a clean kill.

At the end of the day my father-in-law had me shoot the shotgun I'd carried all day. He wanted me to at least shoot it once during that season even though I wouldn't be going back out. He told me to press the shotgun butt firmly against my shoulder because of the strong ricochet. I did as instructed, but the gun still whacked my shoulder pretty hard.

In the end, I was thankful I didn't shoot a deer. It would have been hard, but also there is that Carlson Family rule: "You kill it, you gut it."

For the rest of their hunting times I let the men go out alone, but that entire season I was the only one in the party to have even seen a doe or a valued buck. I overheard talk that having a woman come along in the group—a first for these men—had put a jinx on them all that year. Jinx or not, good-tasting venison or not, I'd rather stay warm at home and leave experienced hunters to do what they do.

Chapter Seventy-three – Tick Tock Ticks

I know they're tiny insects but they still creep me out, mostly because of the fact that they dig into you. Ticks are also arachnids—just a fancy name for spiders.

We usually wear hats or caps while walking through woods in summer (tick season). Sitting in our Michigan backyard underneath the one-hundred-foot tall oak trees often attracted the little darlings—to drop onto me. Didn't matter if I wore a hat or not.

***

When Jeff and I were first married, we'd come home from hikes to do tick checks, making sure we had no hitchhikers crawling over us. The tricky little guys weren't like male mosquitoes who made you aware of their presence. Ticks are silent critters. Although, I've had a number of them crawl over me, I've only ever had one dig into

190

me, on my upper thigh while we were tent camping. Jeff had to encourage it out because I couldn't even look at it digging into my leg.

***

One time on a family camping vacation in Massachusetts, as we watched Peter climb onto the rocks near the shore, I patted John on the top of his three-year-old head. I've always felt patting children's heads was such a demeaning thing to do. In fact, don't recall doing it except for that one time. Undoubtedly it was by God's nudging. When I pat John, I felt something on the top of his head like a huge mole nearly the size of a quarter. Being a conscientious parent, I told him to hold still while I investigated the black object stuck in his black hair. It was a tick, a big, fat, feeding-off-the-head-of-my-child tick.

I relinquished my parental duties to Jeff who encouraged that huge bloodsucker off of our child. Poor John's head bled for a bit. He didn't complain about the "operation." He was only irritated he had to wait until the animal had been removed in order to play along the shore like Peter.

***

I often led the way on hikes. In the Black Hills trails, as per normal Carlson, we'd do a quick tick check at the end of each hike. We climbed over the same fallen trees. We'd marched through the same tall grass. We'd walked beneath the same pines. Yet, by trail's

191

end I was the only Carlson who ever had ticks crawling over her. I assumed they felt the animal heat (me) coming, and all dive-bombed onto the first hot body which passed. The majority probably landed on the ground before the rest of the Carlsons stepped over them. That, or else the tiny black arachnids actually preferred female blood.

Chapter Seventy-four – More Little Guys

We four Carlsons camped once in a private campground in Ontario. It was very expensive, but there wasn't another available campground nearby on our journey. The owner flippantly assured us that his campground was mosquito-free. However, we found that after pitching our tent and eating a quick, simple meal, we couldn't even start a campfire because hordes of insects, which looked and sounded an awfully lot like mosquitoes, descended upon us. It was barely dusk when we crawled in, but the bugs covering our tent made it seem like midnight. We lay side-by-side in our tent, the sound of the amplified buzzing just outside the thin nylon protector keeping us awake. There were so many and so loud, we couldn't even talk over them. We willed ourselves to weigh more so they wouldn't fly our tent away with us inside.

***

Just a P.S. note here about why we don't camp/hike in late spring or early summer: deer flies and black flies. There are two-hundred-and-fifty species of black flies in North America, and they aren't just "up north." The female bite for blood. Black flies don't just sting, but rip off skin to get to the blood below to nourish their eggs. So…ouch. Really. Ouch.

***

My dad had boats since I was seven-years-old. We'd spend summer weekends on Lake Erie. One weekend, we went to one of the Islands where dad anchored off shore for the night. My sister and I decided we wanted to take our sleeping bags and sleep on the beach. Although the waves lapping against the boat used to lull me to sleep, the gentle waves crashing on shore and the clear sky overhead, and being independent from our parents was even better.

In the morning, I awoke to find both my sister's and my sleeping bags covered in black, so many that I couldn't even make out the original color of my sleeping bag. The beach also had small black marks over it. It took me a moment for my awakening brain to figure out what it was: spiders. Yep. Tiny, but mobile spiders.

I screamed and thwacked my sister awake. We struggled out of our sleeping bags, shaking them free of spiders while jumping from one bare foot to the other so they wouldn't climb on us. We both screamed as we rushed into the water holding our bags over our heads where we brushed them into the surf.

193

Mom and Dad stood in the stern of the boat all this time, watching us, not being able to tell why we screamed so and were returning to the boat so early in the morning.

Bette and I never slept on a beach again.

***

The summer after high school graduation my parents, sister, and I took a three-week trip on the Great Lakes with two other families from our marina. Each day we traveled to a new port, noting especially the changes in color between the lakes. Each night the parents gathered on one of the boats to have their adult party, while we five kids would go on one of the other boats and do our own party, ours consisted of card games and Coca-Cola ©.

One night, the parents of the boat we were on returned early and said it was time to break up for the night. Two of the boats shared that same dock. Our boat was tied up at another. When I stepped outside their tarped-for-the-night boat, I found the dock covered with mayflies. The other kids just had to take two steps on the bugs to get to their boat. Not my sister and me. What was worse was that, as per usual, we were bare-footed.

I really didn't want to go all the way down that one dock, across the grass, and up the second dock to our moored boat. I begged to spend the night on our guest's boat, but no. The only way back to ours was on top of the sleeping mayflies. I started out walking slowly feeling the crunches underneath my feet, knowing I was killing every

194

single one I stepped on. After my first three steps, I screamed and ran the rest of the way to our boat, followed close behind by Bette.

In the morning, the mayflies were gone, all except for the dead ones squished on the docks within our outlined footprints.

***

Jeff was involved with the Presbyterian camp in Northwest Iowa on Lake Okoboji. I'd go up with him as often as I could with the boys. We'd walk around the camp while Jeff had his meetings. One fall meeting was during the monarch butterfly migration. There were hundreds and thousands of orange, white, and black monarchs on every tree and bush, and flitting around the air. Monarchs are beautiful individually, but with so many of them, it was surreal. I felt like I was in a dream or in some fantasy world. Absolutely beautiful.

***

Just a note here about outhouse-privy bugs. There are always bugs in outhouses, gnats, flies, mosquitoes, etc. On the rare outhouses, the ones with electric lights attached, at night there are also moths.

One October while in Sleeping Bear Dunes National Lake Shore in Michigan, I was delighted to go inside one to find myself surrounded by dozens of ladybugs. They were flying and crawling. I had to encourage them off the toilet paper roll so I could use some. They made my trip to such a smelly box, delightful.

Moving to the Black Hills of South Dakota gave me an appreciation of rattle snakes. In western South Dakota there are prairie rattlers, which apparently only grow to about 18", although I've seen them bigger.

When you'd hike in the Hills, you must always be aware of where you step, or when rock climbing, be aware of where you place your hand, for snakes like to sun on the warm rocks.

While hiking the Hills with two kids from the church youth group, the boy was ahead of us. Suddenly, I saw him leap up, twist, and I swear he ran on air (without touching ground) to get back to us.

"A rattle. I heard a rattle," he said.

There are specific rules to do when you hear a rattle: 1) stop; 2) identify the location of the sound; and 3) slowly back away.

Of course, there are problems with this, like being too terrified to remember any rules, or like forgetting your environment and running off a cliff, or into knee-high grass where the snaky siblings might be gathered. There's also the knowledge that a snake will only strike as far as the length of its body. But really! Who is going to take the time to measure a curled snake as it's warning you away with its rattle?

Once when the rancher-husband of a writer friend in the Black Hills saw a tornado coming his way, he took refuge under his tracker.

The wife was shocked. "Weren't you afraid of the rattlers?" Apparently, their ranch was covered with the critters. "I was more afraid of the tornado," her husband answered.

An entire hill on the west side of Rapid City was once called Rattlesnake Hill. It's now a subdivision, and occasionally there are still rattlers found in the yards, or garages. One friend tried to urge a rattler out of her garage with a broom. It wasn't cooperating. She called her father-in-law who came right over with a gun and shot it. In the garage. In the city. Welcome to Western South Dakota.

***

Our church music director was a rancher. Keith told me he hated snakes, and won't get off his horse when riding in the Hills. Apparently, everyone knew this. One roundup time, a fellow cowboy was off his horse to…well, relieve himself, and spotted a dead rattler nearby. He grabbed it and kept it hidden until they were on their way again. After a while, the "friend" tossed the snake into Keith's lap on his saddle. Cowboy humor. But not very funny for Keith.

I've mentioned that I was terrified and not terrified of snakes.

As part of a writers group in South Dakota, and being the only children's writer in the group, I started writing adult stories as well. While researching snakes for a story set in Columbia, a place I've never been, I called up the snakiest place I knew: Reptile Gardens. It was wintertime. The wild animal adventure park was closed. But I had questions. The head herpetologist invited me to come to the Gardens to learn more than what was on plaques or in books or on the Internet. As I always prefer real life to book- or video-research, I willingly went.

The guy was amazing, and obviously loved reptiles. As he showed me around, he told me both facts and stories about the snakes there. For instance, he liked to change the bedding in the emerald snakes' cage especially when the front window was crowded with tourists. The snakes, dangling from the cage branches, do not like being disturbed, and would repeatedly strike out and bite him. The tourists screamed. I'm sure I looked horrified. He laughed. "They're not poisonous," he said. "Just grumpy. It doesn't hurt. It's like a cat scratch when you play with it

He had giant cockroaches scurrying over his body as they escaped his hands. He had me pet a beaded lizard (poisonous). He had me hold many kinds of snakes (non-poisonous, of course).

Surprisingly, their scales felt like silk. The more I held, the more my fear melted away.

We went behind the cages to the work areas where there were many trashcan barrels. I figured it was where they stored the barrels for tourist trash...until he opened one. It was half-full of snakes. Snakes are nocturnal and are family animals, liking to curl around each other in a living ball in the dark. They were happy. I was happy when he closed the lid.

Another worker, a man in his 20's, came into the room as my guide took a snake hook from the wall and removed a South American rattle snake from a bin. As he was explaining how it is ten times more poisonous than our South Dakota prairie rattlers and the most dangerous snake in the world, the snake writhed off the hook. I didn't think it could get a grip on the tile floor to move, so stayed put.

I was wrong. That thing twisted and jerked and moved fast!

The other worker jumped onto a waist-high counter, and he was farther from the snake than I was. I remained still, figuring the snake would only go towards moving objects, totally forgetting snakes hunt by heat, like body heat. But my guide, after several tries, finally re-hooked it and returned it to its bin.

Even with that loose Columbian snake experience, by the end of his personal tour, I found totally to my surprise that I was no longer afraid of snakes and was honestly considering getting one as a pet. At least I was never afraid of petting one after that, as long as it was a pet and not startling me in the wild, which still...well, startles me.

Sometime after my Reptile Garden's tour, Jeff was cutting fallen trees off my sister's fence in the Southern Black Hills. There was nothing for me to do but wander the land, which I certainly didn't mind. I started down a ravine. As my hiking stick went into a pile of dead branches, I heard a rattle. I lifted my stick.

Stop. Identify location. Back slowly away.

I stopped, but wasn't quite certain of the snake's location among the dead wood. I placed my stick back into the pile.

Rattle.

I quickly removed my stick, but still couldn't see any movement, nor snake. I put my stick back in.

Rattle.

I grinned. It wasn't attacking, just warning me it was there. I still couldn't see it, but certainly could identify its close proximity. I was fairly sure I hadn't touched it.

One more stick-in-and-rattle, and then I thought it was enough playing with (or irritating) a rattle snake. Poor thing. I looked around to make sure there were no snakes coming to the rescue of the trapped one, then, as the rattle snake rule goes, I backed away.

While hiking in the Black Hills, I (in the lead, of course) spotted this stunningly beautiful green snake sunbathing on our path. I watched it until it slithered away in the grass. It was the most beautiful snake I'd ever seen. The following week we were at the Visitor Center at the Badlands. I asked a ranger about the name of the snake. She didn't know, but pointed me to a book in their store on snakes. It was easy to locate it in the pages, even though the photo didn't do the snake color justice. The name of this green snake? Green snake.

***

One year in the late 1980's I was substitute teaching and assigned to assist the man with animals in the auditorium. At one point, he handed terrified me a snake. I didn't want to scream and run away in front of 150 kids, so I took the snake. Poor thing. I nearly choked it. I also learned that it did not-not-not like my wool sweater. I pulled up my sleeve (still holding tightly near the head) and let him wrap his body around me for warmth. This was winter in New York.

***

About twenty years later, 2017, and well after my Reptile Garden's personal tour, the owner of Critchlow Alligator Sanctuary near Athens, Michigan, came to do a presentation for our church's fall Rally Day.

All of the animals at his sanctuary are rescue animals, i.e., once someone's pet and now no longer wanted. He was quite knowledgeable, of course, and funny. He talked of the four types of reptiles: alligators/crocks/caiman, turtles/tortoises, lizards, and snakes. Of course, he'd saved the "best" creature for the last. When he asked who would like to hold a snake, I shot up my hand. Not surprisingly, no one else raised their hand. He called me up. I took off my sweater on the way because I wanted the snake to feel comfortable against my warm skin. There was some joking about what exactly was I going to do up front, taking off my clothing on the way.

I must admit, after I'd raised my hand to hold the snake, and I then I saw her ample size, I had a moment of nervous regret for volunteering. It had been a long time since I'd handled a snake.

He put the corn snake around my neck and told me I could take her around and show her to people. She didn't stay around my neck for long, but dropped into my arms and hands. I'm thinking my dangling earrings may have bothered her. For a moment, I was afraid I'd drop her on the ground and start a human stampede in that church basement. She was easier to carry in my hands, anyway. I went between the aisles, allowing anyone who wanted to, to pet her. Most people did. People at church called me brave, and I think some who may not have touched a snake before found the courage to do so after they saw their minister's wife holding the snake.

A curious thing I noticed while showing her around was that although mostly the corn snake's tongue stayed in her mouth, when we were near several of the older ladies in the group, the snake's tongue flickered out, smelling the air around them. I figured out, or assumed why this happened. The women were thick with perfume.

Chapter Seventy-nine – Roadkill

Roadkill has always made me sad.

Along the roads I've traveled in various states, I've seen dead dogs, cats, possums, and armadillos. (The latter was in Tennessee.) There've been deer, rabbit, mice, moose, raccoons, skunks, frogs, large turtles, and lots of baby turtles. In Florida there were flattened horseshoe crabs. I imagine the number of animals who crawl off the road to die outnumber those seen along the shoulders.

I know zoos and animal rehab centers take in animals and birds which of been damaged as a result of vehicles on our highways, or unwanted pets.

***

Once when we were going down on the farm, my father saw a small animal on the road. He did not want to swerve to miss it and instead ran over. It was a skunk. It took a couple hours of washing the tires and undercarriage of the car before the skunk smell went away. I'd like to say he refused to swerve because there was oncoming traffic, but there wasn't any.

203

Today the driving rule is, when you see an animal on the road, do not swerve, but hit it, because striking the animal will cause less damage to the people inside or to the vehicle (which could roll to a ravine or crash into a tree, etc). Still…animals and vehicles don't get along well together.

***

When I moved to Wisconsin, especially while driving at night, I'd catch a field mouse making a mad dash across the road just in front of my car and then heard the *tha-whaka-whaka-whaka* as the poor little critter twirled around in the wheel cavity. The first dozen times or so it happened, I'd pull my car to the side of the road searching for the poor field mouse. I never found a single critter.

***

With our roadways racing speeding vehicles, traveling along interstates or backroads have often included daily roadkill sightings of the large beasts. Once while driving through the hills of Pennsylvania, we came to a stretch of about twenty miles where there were fourteen dead deer along the road. Fourteen. After a while I closed my eyes (Jeff was driving).

***

We Carlsons Four stopped at Hell's Half Acre, Wyoming, to find a bird embedded in the grill of our van.

***

204

Oh. And then there is East River, South Dakota.

When driving the boys to college seven hours away (or visiting them), all through West River country our windshields would be clear. But when we reached the Missouri River dividing the state from prairie land into farmland. After that, bug spats. We literally had to fill up with more windshield wiper fluid after each visit east. Apparently, bugs like the moist farm crops to the east better than prairie grass to the west.

***

One very sad walk was at the Leila Arboretum in Battle Creek. Jeff and I had gone down the road walking towards the creek area when we came across a smooshed baby turtle, about one inch in diameter. As we walked on, to my horror, there were about a dozen smooshed baby turtles on the road. I now can't say "baby turtles" without thinking of all those crushed shells.

Chapter Eighty – The Other Snakes and Such

As I've mentioned, from when I was a child, snakes have been a constant in my life. When we hike in the fall, a time when snakes really ought to be sleeping in these northern regions, every once in while I spot one shooting off under the leaves at my feet. Of course, I jump, even though I realize mid-air that it's just a stick snake.

Literally, a stick. I can't help my startled response as it "slithers" off in front of me every time I kick one.

The same thing will happen on winter hikes with their cousins, the snow snakes. There they go scooting beneath the snow right by my feet in front of me, and there I go leaping into the air.

All right. So, these aren't living snakes, but we call them stick snakes and snow snakes, anyway, especially because they move the same and get the same reaction out of me as real ones.

There is another creature "out there" which we looked for as kids, and later tried to find with younger kids or youth. Since I don't know where else to include this animal, they go here: Snipes. That's right. I've been on many a Snipe Hunt with flashlight, through the fields, through the woods, around the edges of lakes. And, sad to say, after all those times searching, I have yet to spot a single one.

Chapter Eighty-one – More Encounters

Each time I think I'm finished writing up my past animal encounters, a week later I am reminded of yet another influential, very obvious one I'd forgotten, like one Easter down on the farm, us three Stark kids getting dyed chicks and "forgetting" to bring them home to the city. We couldn't wait until the next visit to find our pink, green, and blue chickens. Disappointingly, they were all white, with no distinguishing marks.

When we lived in Western New York, people were getting sick, and some even dying, from ticks giving them Lyme disease. Then we moved to Western South Dakota where we went through several years of drought. Living in the bracken waters left behind, drew fourteen species of mosquitoes which carried the West Nile Virus. Many people in western South Dakota contracted this disease. Some "merely" got the fever and survived. Others died. Everyone in the state (including us) knew someone who was infected or died from it, because sparsely-populated South Dakota happens to be a small town with very long roads. There are only two degrees of separation there.

I wrote a chapter on neglected and abused animals, and consequently deleted it. It was too sad to include.

There are also several one-sentence encounters, like the irritating alarm clock of a single mosquito at your ear, and then slapping yourself hard while half-asleep intending to kill it...and missing.

We've seen many 4-H animal antics at fairs, including Dash for the Mash, and Stock Shows.

There was the boy on an Iowa church youth group picnic to a lake who climbed back on the church bus with his pockets and pants stuffed with forty-one very large and wiggling bull frogs.

While teaching in Illinois, I took my students to watch a herd of sheep being sheered by professional (and fast) hands. Slick.

Once I sat in our Michigan backyard and was startled by a black squirrel about three feet from me, who was then started by my yelp, at which time he leapt three feet straight up into the air before vanishing into the bushes.

There were the chickadees we Carlsons hand-fed in Fireman's Park in Cheektowaga, New York.

I had the honor to watch a mama red-tailed hawk in South Dakota feeding her Baby Hewey chick, nearly twice her size, who wobbled precariously on a telephone wire. And there was the red-tailed hawk family in Michigan who remained with me during the horrid summer after the storm destroyed our house and yard.

I held a stinky spider monkey in Honduras, and got poo-ed down my back by a macaw sitting on my shoulder.

I helped Rosie do hog chores in Wisconsin, so we could spend Friday evenings "playing" down in Madison.

There are the beautiful migrating sandhill cranes in Michigan with their long legs, unique coloration and haunting cries as they fly or wander cornfields with their chicks, usually two adults and two chicks per sighting.

While boating a narrow channel, we've seen numerous turtles on logs. We've seen deer there, but once we saw a sandhill crane on the lawn near the bank when a great blue heron swooped in and passed between us.

There've been encounters with humming birds, box-elder and stink bugs, big horn sheep, Japanese beetles, the squirrel with white ears we named Blondie, a spider dangling over a woman's head in front of me at a Chautauqua concert, marmots, elk, precious fox sightings, opossums, the strange-looking skunk we urged out from our garage, mites, mountain goats, prairie dogs, and so many more.

These stories here are not exhaustive, and I hope for many more experiences to come with our wild and domesticated "cousins," both for us and for our descendants.

I pray, too, that you readers are able to experience and enjoy your own animal adventures in God's great creation.

Be wise. Stay safe.

Re: the bumble bee shot on the back-cover

If you thought there'd be a story about bumblebees because of the photo, there obviously wasn't. Although I've seen many of them, I have no interesting stories involving these creatures, except that, similar to the unicorn, they seem to be a scientific impossibility—the bees with their heavy bodies and tiny wings, and the unicorns with their incredible stealth skills.